THE MENOPAUSE
MILLIONAIRE

CAROLE HODGES

Winsome Entertainment Group LLC

Menopause Millionaire

Carole Hodges
PO Box 2191
Fallbrook, CA 92088
Carole@Carolehodges.com

Ordering Information:

Special discounts are available on quantity purchases by corporations, associations, educational institutions, and others. For details, contact Carole Hodges above.

Printed in the United States of America

First Edition

ISBN 978-1-5136-9100-8

Publisher: Winsome Entertainment Group LLC

Testimonials

"The Menopause Millionaire is an inspiring and timely discussion for women facing mid-life changes and seeking a solid financial future. I enjoyed the engaging stories and insightful questions that gave me a path to my future."

~Dame Michelle Patterson, President of The California Women's Conference

"I thoroughly enjoyed this fresh approach to the meaning of menopause and life change. I'm delighted that more and more mid-life women are stepping up as leaders and bringing wisdom to business, society, and nations worldwide. The Menopause Millionaire is a thought-provoking self-examination that offers readers both clarity and purpose. I love this book!"

~Paula Fellingham, Founder of www.WinWinWomen.com - A Global Women's Movement of Caring, Connection, and Collaboration.

"Thank you Carole for a much needed book! What I love about this book is that the underlying message to women is to learn to trust ourselves. We need both our heads and our hearts to thoroughly investigate our choices. Follow Carole's sage advice and guidance and trust yourself. This book is a perfect balance of wisdom and practicality."

~Deborah Smith Founder & CEO, Rewardify Inc.

Contents

Dedication

I dedicate this book to my husband, Paul Schumann. He is my greatest fan. He has made magic to bring this effort to life.

I also dedicate my work to my children. You are champions who walked the bumpy road with me and have your own stories to tell.

Acknowledgements

First, I thank my dear friend, Liz Jamieson Dunne, who provided encouragement and feedback to keep me going. My book whisperer, Jared Rosen, convinced me time and time again that I was creating valuable and fun content for my readers. He saved me from terminal self-doubt! My editor, Kristy Boyd Johnson, is a kindred spirit of positive change. Thank you for handling the details that I missed.

Juliet Clark, my publisher, took the wheelbarrow of tasks and gave them to me one at a time. The impossible became easy! Juliet's team at Winsome Entertainment Group surprised me with stellar and delightful graphics. I love their creativity!

I also acknowledge my friends and colleagues from Tribeup.com and JVology. Having a team of friends ready to share and support my book is a special gift. I thank you for your trust and love. You boost my spirits and lift me up.

And thank you to the many long time friends who participated in my life. I cherish your friendship and support. Special thanks to those of you who fed me and passed the Kleenex when I needed it most. I love you forever.

Foreword

For the past 42 years, I have had the honor and privilege of being around the entrepreneurial-experiential-transformational industry as I shared my *Money & You®* programs, along with the *Excellerated Business School for Entrepreneurs®*, and Excellerated events. My experience with tens of thousands of participants has given me an understanding of what women go through when they have not had a practical financial literacy education. These women are not at fault because educational systems worldwide do not teach people how to prepare for the second half of life or, as I prefer to call it, the "second surge of life."

I refer to the prediction of the great R. Buckminster Fuller and the ripple effect of various diseases around the world. Scientists are urgently creating breakthrough products to improve our health and well-being. Buckminster Fuller's last prediction appears imminent – he made over 50 predictions (primarily mathematical – ever heard of "Buckyballs?"). Only this one hasn't come true. He said that if you were under 40 years old in 1970 and didn't smoke, your life expectancy could be up to 140 years old.

Anticipating this longevity, I take care of myself physically, emotionally, spiritually, mentally, and of course, financially. The question is, "What happens if we are not prepared?" A book like Carole's can become a valuable resource.

I experienced significant changes and challenges in what would be called my mid-life. I was 44 years old when I got married for the first time. I brought my business, network, reputation, worldwide contacts, and a million dollars cash into the relationship. We built a substantial business in Singapore until the Asian Financial Crisis of '97/'98. Many Americans are not familiar with this massive crisis that shook the entire Asia Pacific region to its economic core – and the business we had so successfully created disappeared in one week. There was nothing anyone could do to prevent it. Along with a million others, I found myself in debt for half a million dollars (too long of a story of how I was left "holding the bag," so to speak).

Since I had never been in debt, it was very tough. Until then, I had never understood why people jump off buildings when they lose all their money, or their businesses. I didn't know that it isn't just about the money – it's the emotional toll it takes to get yourself out of a financial hole. The regret, the shame, the guilt – the constant "what could I have done differently" nagging in your head can drive anybody nuts. I, along with many others, didn't know how to handle it emotionally. I was blessed to have friends who recommended that I get expert advice. One friend recommended a debt negotiator, Paul Schumann, who supported me by traveling with me to AsiaPac. He helped negotiate for me. He was there for advice and to hold my hand as I was emotionally recuperating.

I was very blessed because I had homes in Hawaii and San Diego, California, even though I lived in Singapore. My programs are global. When I returned to the United States, I could re-establish my business faster because the financial world was undisturbed there. Because I had tools and systems, I knew my plan. We teach the same tools in *Money & You*, our *Business Schools*, and other *Excellerated* programs. I also had my network, contacts, and business models, and I owned the intellectual rights. My access to support, experts, and knowledge provided support to get me back on my feet. In a couple of years, I was back, and with all my learning experiences, I was able to rebuild our global organization better than ever (with the support of fabulous partners and team).

Change is a certainty of life. The unexpected will happen, often when you are not prepared. Carole's personal stories, and those of other women, put change in perspective. We can sometimes prepare, yet we also need to find the inner strength – and the support – to deal with the unimaginable.

Carole has spent many years studying the principles of success in both life and business. She blends the wisdom of masters with practical steps for directing your health, relationships, and financial life. I have known her as both a financial professional and as a friend.

Carole's core family also surrounds her with knowledgeable people. Her husband, who has been a constant pillar of support to me for over two decades, is masterful in real estate, legalities, and debt reduction. Her brother, Roger Herrick, is a master of real estate finance. I love that Carole has distilled some of the best strategies, technologies, and tools to help you quickly get the financial basics down and accelerate your learning process to be more fully prepared for what is to come.

The *Menopause Millionaire* is a valuable companion for celebrating the second half of life with joy and resilience – and for some of you, the "second third of your life." Read on!

~Dame Doria (DC) Cordova, Ph.D. (Hon.)
CEO / Owner, Excellerated Business Schools for Entrepreneurs / Money & You
www.MeetDoria.com

Introduction

I began writing this book as a modern financial fable to improve the lives of many women readers. At age 50, I tripped into one of life's financial potholes. I suddenly doubted my earlier belief that I was a smart woman. I made numerous dumb financial choices before climbing out of the mud and recharting my life map. I learned a better way that fortified my determination to save other women from avoidable pain.

Technology brings change at an accelerating rate. Only the foolhardy would predict what our lives will be like ten or twenty years from now. Yet if you are a woman at mid-life, the "change" means only one thing...YES, your body is changing, giving up the fertility and energy of youth, and entering a new era of life. Menopause could be an easy transition, or it may rock your world, giving you a new perspective and transforming the younger you into a mighty, self-expressed maven of wisdom.

The transition of menopause is both inevitable and mysterious. It is unavoidable because it is part of our human experience and the undeniable sign of female aging. You notice a few silver hairs, wrinkles begin to creep in near your eyes, and then WHAM...you find yourself with the irritability of hot flashes.

Mysteriously, you also begin to acknowledge that life's experience has provided you with a most welcome perspective of wise detachment. Minor irritations that once caused you concern have lost their grip. Perhaps the crumbs left by your grandchild or the dog hair on the sofa become a regular part of your home. You might even discover a new appreciation of your nosy neighbor who stops you on the way to your car.

Yes, life is changing. You are changing. The world is changing. This time, this moment, is your pivot point. You are the captain of your ship. Many years ago, I learned to master a sailboat. Sailing is not a solo endeavor; it is a partnership with nature. While I might have controlled my boat's condition, direction, and the set of my sails, I was never entirely in charge of the experience. Wind, weather, the volatility of the sea, and my crew's skill and determination were not mine to command. I have traveled on calm, windless seas, and confronted waves that could have swamped my boat. I have fought both boredom and self-doubt. I learned that the worst thing to do in a storm is panic. When confronted with adversity, we must gather our wits and skills while hoping for a bit of luck. Our lives are like a journey on the open sea. We can check the map, set the compass, monitor the sails, and guide the wheel, yet our life experiences and destinations are not within our control.

At mid-life, we have gained experience by making choices. Some were wonderful, while others were humbling, painful, or humiliating. What I know is that we have acquired stamina and wisdom along the way. We have learned to think on our feet.

And we are curious how to prepare for the next leg of the journey.

If you picked up this book for yourself – I suspect you have reached mid-life. Your life experience has built both your strengths and your blind spots. You have faced storms and learned survival skills that have given you a sense of who you are. If you are honest, you also doubt yourself. You may contemplate past choices and future possibilities. How do I know? Because you are human, you have an internal voice questioning your choices. Because you are a woman, you connect with others at home and work. As women, we create a human community for mutual support. This life journey is one constant game of discovery. Now you are at a pivot point. Mid-life is the time to check your compass and draw a new path on your map as you move toward the culmination of your remarkable life.

I am writing this book as the guide I wish I had years ago. I made mistakes that I might have avoided. I've learned along the way and continue to learn. I see the second half of life as a beautiful opportunity to learn while stepping into the wisdom which becomes possible when we are open, willing, and conscious of the miracle of life.

This book has three sections that encompass the fullness of life – Body, Mind, and Spirit.

• **Part ONE – LIFE IN YOUR BODY.** We begin by examining where you are in your life. How do you struggle with your body, relationships, and self-image?

• **Part TWO – MIND YOUR MONEY.** In this section, we introduce money structure in your life. We do not make recommendations, nor do we become an encyclopedia of financial wisdom. Our goal is not to provide you with specific solutions but to inspire you to create a checklist for further exploration. Do NOT skip this section. If you review your financial options at age 50, you can shift your future. If you read this at 65 or 70, it is too late for you to benefit from many of these options.

• **Part THREE – OPEN YOUR SPIRIT**. In this section, we address the challenges of our society and time of life. What do you believe now? How do you face a world of accelerating change? What is necessary to live a life that gives you satisfaction and completion?

Getting the sweetest juice from life begins with self-reflection. Take this opportunity for a deep dive into yourself. As you go through this book, you will find reflection exercises at the end of each chapter. Spend time on these. You can come back to them in your own time. You might choose to journal or to discuss with friends.

My wish is for you to uncover new possibilities and potential which you previously ignored or set aside. Could NOW be the perfect time to grow and discover?

Part One

LIFE IN YOUR BODY

"Take care of your body. It's the only place you have to live."

~Jim Rohn

Chapter One

YOUR PIVOT POINT

"The great thing about getting older is that you don't lose all the other ages you've been."
~Madeleine L'Engle

ONE DAY UPON WAKING, I looked in the mirror. Looking back at me was a woman who was no longer young. She had a few creases between her brows and an air of experience.

Although I had comforted my face with creams and colors every day, today was different. Experience and the unavoidable hints of aging stared back at me. In truth, nothing was vastly different from the day before. Yet, everything was shifting. My periods were erratic, sometimes skipping, sometimes flowing for two weeks.

"Perfectly normal," said my doctor.

I accepted the change without drama, having learned that struggling against the inevitable makes one cranky.

I didn't FEEL old. I didn't ACT old. I'm still ready to conquer challenges and explore new adventures. Then it hit me. I was starting the SECOND half of life. Intuitively, I knew that more than my body was changing. I was shifting direction.

If you are a woman who is approaching menopause, you see change everywhere. Your children step into adult responsibilities while your body rebels like a teenager. You are ready to overhaul your very identity.

Then comes menopause – the word has different emotional meanings to every woman. Your body stops your monthlies, PERIOD. You can no longer get pregnant and have babies. Perhaps this is a welcome relief. OR you may suddenly be mourning a loss or possibly acknowledging that you forgot to have children.

If you are already a post-menopausal woman, you may remember that bright-eyed girl who once dreamed of her future. A well-earned sense of wisdom has replaced her dreams. Through triumphs and losses, you have learned to feel deeply and to care from your core. You have become a unique WOMAN.

In the pages that follow, we will be discussing money and what it means to you. You may be surprised at what you learn. Money has a unique meaning to everyone. You can easily observe differences in the ways people spend, save, work, and play. Each of us has our idea of what is appropriate. You might spend hundreds of dollars on a special dinner with friends, or you might buy an outfit for more than a thousand dollars. Or you might find both of those ideas an incomprehensible waste. Your attitude is not predictable by how much money you have or earn. Your feelings about money are your own.

Money is a form of energy. Money is emotional. Even when

you learn sound money management principles, you will never feel satisfied unless you navigate your money map. Diving into your feelings is essential. You must recognize your money energy before you set sail to discover a new world of financial freedom in the second half of life. You have the power to create what you want. When you uncover your feelings, you can make changes that empower you. Money habits that may have enslaved you in the past can be changed and allow you the freedom to choose again. New money habits become easy when you include the fresh energy of fun and self-fulfillment.

I did not recognize the energy of money early in life. I was always fiscally responsible, kept track of money, and shopped wisely. Family and friends offered me jobs, so I never searched for opportunities. I was almost fifty before I composed my first employment resume. Although my life looked easy on the outside, I spent years fumbling in the dark financially.

I graduated from college with a major in English Literature and Philosophy. My father hired me to assist in his insurance office. Then I worked with my ex-husband in several businesses, including an early computer services company, running a wind park, fulfilling government contracts, and monitoring limited partnerships. I learned Quicken and QuickBooks to track multiple corporations and the family budget. Details surrounded me at every turn. I learned corporate accounting, paid taxes, negotiated contracts, and met with clients. I did it all while I raised children, attended soccer games, and volunteered for school programs. My title was Vice-President of our company. It sounds glamorous, but the title had no functional meaning. I couldn't imagine that any other company would be impressed enough to hire me as the vice president of anything.

I thought I knew quite a lot about money, especially since I paid bills and tracked all money flow at home and in the office. But in my mind, money was only a form of math.

At the same time, I was active in my community. I wrote about a dozen women's club shows to raise money for my church. I learned to dance jazz, tap, and ballet, studied voice and acting, and performed in local musicals for fun.

I kept myself very busy. As I approached fifty, my life was shifting. My marriage was falling apart. I was working with my husband, but money was scarce. I began to look for a job to pay for groceries.

It was a moment of truth. In the middle of my life, I had no idea how to describe my skill set. I never thought about this before. I simply learned new things and did them. I was clueless about defining my skills or having confidence in what I should earn. Looking for a job was an "Alice in Wonderland" mystery. I had no idea what kind of a job I wanted.

I signed up with a temporary agency to earn while I was job-hunting. In these gigs, I made only enough for my family's weekly groceries. I found the work easy. I usually worked efficiently and found myself sitting at a desk with nothing to do after completing my daily assignments. I studied tutorials on Excel, Word, and PowerPoint to fill the time. I learned quite a bit during this extra time on temp jobs.

I suspect that my experience is not unusual. If you have put aside your professional development to focus on the well-being of your children and family, you may have lost a sense of your economic value. No one awards bonuses and commendations for motherhood skills. You might qualify as an elite strategist, proficient in psychology, home decorating, nutrition, and education. If you can persuade a child to complete their homework and chores without argument, you have the finesse of a top-notch salesperson!

What are your skills? Do you truly know your value? How do you define money-worthy skills? Love, compassion, contribution, and influence are valuable. That brings us to another related discussion. How can we combine a life that we love with financial compensation that allows us to thrive?

How Much Money Do You Need to Be Happy?

We all want enough money to be happy. While money cannot MAKE you happy, the lack of money causes stress. Some academic researchers have wondered, "Is there a perfect money balance where you can relax and enjoy life?"

In 2008-2009, some Princeton researchers gathered poll data from Gallup researchers (Belinda Luscombe, "Do We Need $75,000 a Year to Be Happy?" Time Magazine, September 06, 2010). First they asked whether a person was more content when their income doubled. Most people claimed they were happier with each doubling of their income yet admitted additional stress and time pressure.

The researchers dug deeper. They wanted to uncover the magic income, which increased satisfaction without adding stress. Their second question was more targeted.

They asked respondents to assess their happy hours in the previous days. Specifically, they wanted to know whether people had experienced a lot of enjoyment, laughter and smiling. They also measured their anger, stress, and worry. Using this new "happiness measure," they found that money mattered only up to about $75,000.

Ten years later, in 2018, Andrew T. Jebb, a doctoral student at Purdue University, conducted another study of happiness and money (Andrew T. Jebb, Louis Tay, Ed Diener, and Shigehiro Oishi, "Happiness, Income Satiation and Turning Points Around the World" Abstract, Purdue University February 13, 2018). He made two distinctions regarding happiness. He measured "emotional well-being," which he described as feelings that include day-to-day emotions, such as feeling happy, excited, sad, and angry. Jebb also monitored "life evaluation," which is a measure of self-satisfaction. "Life evaluation" is a measure of comparison with others, while "well-being" is an internal measure.

Jebb concluded that the ideal income for positive "life evaluation" was $95,000, while an income of $60,000 to $75,000 was sufficient for "well-being." These 2018 amounts are not fixed and will differ by location and cost of living. Income totals were for single individuals and would likely be higher for families. The conclusion is that money CAN contribute to your sense of well-being, yet counting your **happy hours** provides the most accurate measure of happiness and satisfaction with life.

There are several points to take away:

1. Finding your "happy money" target is not an exact science. Inflation and the cost of living vary. You CAN achieve an amount of money to live a happy life. The good news is that you decide the exact amount for yourself.
2. Happiness is an inside job, and it does take time. How much time per day or week will you devote to

your happiness? Have you been paying attention to
your happiness?

Happy moments are the real treasure of human life, yet how
few of us track smiles and good feelings as a measure of our
quality of life? Naturally, there can be distress when we earn too
little. But what about the stress potential of making too much?
As you move into the second half of your life, you may be
asking another question: "How do I ensure that I can earn my
'happy income' throughout my retirement?"

Lynne Twist, author of *The Soul of Money* (W.W. Norton &
Company, Copyright 2003) makes a case for the concept of
"profound sufficiency," or precisely enough money. Achieving
this mythical amount and not striving for more "frees up
immense energy to make a difference with what you have."

Money is full of myth, mystery, and emotion. When you
have the perfect amount of money in your life, providing the
maximum of daily happy moments, it frees immense energy to
make a difference. Start by examining your thoughts and feelings and counting your happy moments. You can use a scientific
approach if you track your observations in your daily journal.

As you enter the second half of life, you will benefit by
determining your "happy money" number. Entering retirement,
you could plan a life with enough money to be happy as long as
you live. If you are earning more than "profound sufficiency,"
this is a good time to invest in a lifelong flow of income that
keeps you truly happy.

The Game of Life

Imagine for a moment that we have a board game in front of us. Perhaps it is the game of Monopoly that has been popular for more than a century. Each player chooses their plastic game piece and follows the rules of the game. Of course, any player is free to walk away, toss their player piece across the room, or declare herself the winner on the second roll of the dice. When we play a game, we do not lose our "real life" capabilities. The rules allow us to have fun and adventure. Our triumphs and disappointments are exciting. A player could become a financial tycoon or wind up in jail with the throw of the dice. We play games to enjoy the mental challenge and share time with friends. Uncertainty is part of the fun! At the end of the game, players can laugh it off until they decide to return for another round.

What if your life is also a game? Let's stretch your spiritual beliefs and imagine your existence before this earthly adventure. What if we came here from that same Heaven where we return after death? You don't have to agree with me. Just investigate your faith for answers. If you believe in Heaven, then you believe in a life after this human experience. What if God cared so much that he gave you specific parents? What if your unborn spirit requested a particular experience in this lifetime? While I don't claim any esoteric knowledge, the thought that life might be a game makes me smile whenever I'm surprised by the twists and turns of everyday living.

Wouldn't that be a wild ride? What if our human existence is the opportunity to play the Life on Earth Game? Welcome to my "cosmic game board" theory of life. Could each of us have released the *limitless power of spirit* to play our "human game?" The rules are the same for each of us. While here, we follow the human rules: we live sequentially, with a past, present, and future; our bodies need food and sleep; we reproduce by connecting with another human of the opposite sex; we can only be in one place at a time; we require money to obtain necessities; most of us work to get it. These rules govern our life here on earth, and we take them for granted. We even add silly rules, like never wearing white before Easter.

Some people decide that those with the most money and stuff win the game. While this isn't true for everyone, you may want to examine your rules. In human life, a person might have a stretch of bad luck. In Monopoly, they could land in jail, but it would be crazy for a player to give up and decide they will never win. A game player knows it is just a game. They can have more fun by starting again and enjoying the throw of the dice. You can even change the rules a bit. What if you played the game so that no one wins unless everyone wins? Imagine a different outcome for our game!

The real question is: how can you make your life the most fantastic game you will ever play? Could it be all about the adventure? God, Spirit, or Universe are watching over you and always there to support you. When you bring your talents and wisdom to the game, it is fun! Your goal is to be happy and enjoy the experience. When you connect with other people, you spread love and joy. Everything you learn on Earth brings all of us a step closer to winning. We may not be able to prove it scientifically, but it is a good thought.

I have always been a lifelong learner and enjoy thinking about how the future expands knowledge through science. One scientific theory is that time and matter are flexible, and our universe is constantly growing. This theory proposes that a journey of a billion miles might be traveled in seconds when time folds upon itself. Other research demonstrates that we can change our bodies and even our reality using our thoughts and expectations. What if this and much more is possible? As we journey together, I invite you to expand what is possible for you.

What is a Menopause Millionaire?

Rarely is "menopause" followed by "millionaire." I was attending a business seminar when the title of this book was "downloaded" to me. I was contemplating a name for a new program when I received a sudden burst of inspiration that made me smile.

I give credit for the name to the spirit genie sending me a message. As I pondered a name for my financial program for women, the words "Menopause Millionaire" popped into my head, and I giggled. The following day when I announced my "Menopause Millionaire program," women smiled, applauded, and let out a sigh of relief as though I had unearthed a well-deserved mid-life award. Women responded to the promise of a prize at mid-life and acknowledgment for their well-traveled road to wisdom through experience.

Men had a different response. They felt excluded from our special secret. Upon hearing the word "menopause," men would shift uncomfortably in their chairs. One man was adamant that I should remove the word "menopause" and include the men. I sense that men struggle with aging as much as we do. While men may not experience "the change," they want to learn our money secrets.

However, my intent is not for this book to become another generic guide to investment and retirement. There are plenty of books that can give you the dynamics of investing and various strategies for retirement. This book is addressed to women because we can change the way the world works. Women have become a significant part of the workforce. In the 1950s, the stay-at-home mom was standard. If you are heading into retirement soon, your mother may have been a full-time mom. By the 1970s, women expected and even demanded equal income, as well as responsibility. Women today have learned to balance the competing responsibilities of both work and parenthood. This book is for you – "The Menopause Millionaire."

What does the word "millionaire" mean today? At one time, anyone calling herself a millionaire was lush with luxury and flush with cash. You know the feeling. Imagine having a million dollars in the bank and credit cards that allow you to buy whatever your heart desires. Historically (in other words, when I was twenty years old),), a million dollars was a lot of money. In my younger years, prices were vastly different. I recall when an average starter house in California was $25,000. And you could purchase a NEW 4-door Mercedes sedan for $7,800. (I have done that!)

Today, our financial perspective has changed. While a yearly salary of $1,000,000 is still out of reach for most people, the value of money has changed. If you are reading this book, you have had a million dollars flow through your fingers during your lifetime. Have you earned an average income of $34,000 over the last 30 years? Or have you directed your household finances over the years? If the answer is yes, then you can legitimately call yourself a millionaire. You have distributed $1,000,000 of personal wealth. Does that make you feel rich? Or are you questioning where it all went?

Let's call this "cash flow." Money is not a static commodity. Even when you are not earning or spending money, you have the potential to "grow" as well as to "lose" money through investments, inflation, and interest. How you use your money may result in positive or negative outcomes. Think of how you earn, spend, save, invest, or share through gifts and donations. How did each decision impact you? Are you beginning to see the importance of understanding money?

In mid-life, you have significant decisions to make. You have reached the intermission separating the first and second acts of life. Imagine watching a captivating play or musical. By the end of the first act, you have met the players and engaged with their challenges. Each person confronts a crisis. After a short break, you rush to your seat for an exciting conclusion. Intermission allows you to get a snack, share your thoughts with friends, and imagine the outcome.

Let this book be your "intermission." Acknowledge and reflect on your accomplishments, your disappointments, and what you have learned in the process. Now imagine the adventures you could encounter before the curtain drops.

Congratulations on recognizing that YOU ARE A MILLIONAIRE! Since you have already handled a million dollars – what can you expect in your future?

Once you reach 50, you might reasonably expect to live an additional 30 to 50 years. How much money will you need for the remainder of your life? Might that figure be more than a million? You probably recognize an uncomfortable truth. A million dollars will only provide you with a modest lifestyle. If your total savings is $150K, you will have to make significant changes. You can either lower your expectations or raise your resolve and intention to create the lifestyle and contribution that matches your vision.

Now is time for a wake-up call. Just as your body is announcing THE CHANGE, your financial awareness may need a good kick in the savings account. Remember that since YOU have already handled a million dollars, you have the skills to do it again, and you have a mature perspective. Together, we'll explore ideas and information that will assist you in your choices.

In this book, you will find some elementary education about financial options. There are guides to social security, life insurance, real estate, annuities, and long-term care insurance. While the factual nature of these topics may not intrigue you, I urge you to learn how these financial tools could impact your future. At age 50, these are worthwhile and valuable choices for some of you. At age 70, these will no longer be viable choices because you will not qualify for coverage; the cost will have become prohibitive, and you may wish you had paid attention earlier.

Your life is an adventurous journey. You can evaluate the past and design what is to come. By educating yourself on financial options, you can plan a meaningful future. If you ignore the warning signs at this monetary junction, you may fall into the canyon of despair. Or you may grow your financial wings and fly. (Envision a butterfly and SMILE!!)

Why is Money a Critical Topic at Menopause?

There is ONE central message in this book: TIME AND MONEY ARE PARTNERS IN CREATING YOUR FUTURE. It would be best if you had time to grow savings into a pool of money to sustain you in the second half. Like you, I heard this message, but I ignored it. You have probably seen projections for a 20-year-old who saves 10% of her income until retirement. Amazingly, her relatively modest monthly contributions amount to a million dollars or more at retirement. It is not magic; it is the reliable result of compound interest. When I turned 50, I began to view this type of reminder as simply annoying. I will never be 20 again. I'm glad I will never be 20 again. I'd hate to relinquish the vast experience and the gems of wisdom I've gained over the years. On the other hand, I have lost the opportunity to contribute 10% of a modest income and grow it into financial security in my older years. At menopause, you do not have this opportunity either.

My intent is not to deflate you. I want to wake you up. When you become aware of the time already passed and how quickly you step into your future, you recognize the importance of every decision you make NOW! This one red flag of warning is my reason for writing this book. At mid-life, you are making irreversible choices with money. If you ignore the importance of time for financial growth, you could shackle yourself to a lifetime of working and penny-pinching. The current statistics of retirement savings are dismal. The average 50-year-old American has $175,510 saved for retirement. (Kathleen Elkins "Here's how much money Americans have in savings at every income level" MONEY, September 27, 2018). And the median

American household savings is $11,700. Experts recommend personal savings of six to seven times your annual income by age 50. If you are currently earning $60,000 per year, your savings by age 50 should be $360-420,000.

If you are at this level of savings, I applaud you! Keep up the excellent work! And pay attention to ways that you can protect your nest egg. If you are not at this level, I fully understand. I was starting over from ground zero when I turned 50. In fact, I had to imagine that I was 20 as a trick to raise my spirits.

You can discover resilience and courage in the face of obstacles. In the second half of life, you may need even more courage than the first half. Life will continue to be just as mysterious as before. Despite your many years of experience, life still drops both pebbles and boulders in your path to trip you up or halt your progress. We all have lessons to learn as long as we are breathing. I believe that women need to take leadership in using money wisely.

If you want to jump right to the chapters about money, feel free to review these first. I will not be giving you the secret keys to building up your fortune. Life is not a game show with the grand prize behind doors 1, 2, or 3. Instead, you will learn the principles behind various investments and financial options you might use to fund your later years. My goal is to be objective with a broad stroke. Every choice has both an upside and a downside. I suggest you read this section several times. First, get a general overview and decide which areas are of interest or concern for you.

Begin by taking a personal inventory of your assets and liabilities. Get the details of your bank accounts, investments, insurance, and any other sources of income and expense. If you are expecting an inheritance, list that as well. While you are listing assets, include your possessions: your home, real estate, furniture, cars, jewelry. And finally, list your skills and talents. Too often, we ignore our human treasures, which are the underlying sources of our wealth. Your ability to earn, lead, care for others, and live a life rich in experience and expression is your true wealth.

As we journey together, you will find tools to support you in taking your life and wealth inventory. I recommend keeping a simple notebook handy for your observations. You are likely to remember important moments in your life that you want to explore further. If you are typical, your financial life co-mingles with others. Take notes in your journal as you notice the dynamic network behind your financial decisions.

Both menopause and money are emotional topics. We have deep feelings about our health and wealth, which flow into our feelings of self-worth and impact our life experience. My goal for our time together is to uncover the root of everything - your life purpose. By mid-life, caring for others or building your career success may have buried your unique life mission. Your one wonderful life is an adventure. It is your journey in time and space that began with God, spirit, and universal wisdom. Your human body combines trillions of cells, working together. You are a being in a physical and energetic world of possibility. In our life adventure, we never know what surprises await around the very next corner. What appears to be a disaster might open the door to something extraordinary. Life is an adventure when you are open to finding wonder in each moment. I support you in creating an experience worth living.

KEYS FOR REFLECTION:

1. What are your thoughts and feelings about aging?
2. What will be different when you are "old?" At what age does this happen?
3. Name a few women that you admire. What have they accomplished that is worthy of admiration? How old are they?

Chapter Two

EXPLORING YOUR JOURNEY

"If you don't change direction, you may end up where you are heading."
    ~Lao Tzu

IT MAY SEEM that everything is falling apart as your body shifts. At the same time, pieces of your life are falling together as your authentic self emerges. How do you manage these seemingly conflicting energies? Reflect on your life before this moment. Were you a mother engulfed in raising children? As your children grow into adulthood, your earlier role is obsolete. Your children are free to claim their independent identities. From their perspective, you may have become the village dunce OR the Yoda of wisdom. I have often felt like both!

I remember a discussion with my youngest daughter when she was thirteen years old. She was upset with me and proclaiming that I had NO idea about life. I smiled as I remembered her older sister giving me the very same lecture. I apologized to her, saying, "I'm sorry, but this has happened before. When one of my children turns thirteen, I seem to get very stupid. I have heard that, by the time you are thirty, I will get smart again. If you are patient with me, we can both get through this together." She was still irritated, but I felt better.

At this critical mid-point in your life, you can definitively claim your identity. It can be a wild ride! Imagine yourself in Disneyland. Perhaps you were on Space Mountain and then headed for the Jungle Cruise. Now is time for a change of energy and focus.

What is Happening to Your Mind and Body?

If you are actively going through menopause, be BRAVE! Your body can be rebellious. One moment you feel ice-cold shivers followed by a roasting sensation. HOT FLASHES! No one can prepare you for this rotating urgency which can be as ridiculous as a sitcom. I ran a repetitive marathon of sweater antics. One moment I would feel like I was sitting in a freezer. After frantically pulling on a sweater, I would have a moment of relief. Then I could feel the room filling with hot steam. Forgetting my recent shock of icy cold, I found myself dripping, soaked, and miserable. Ripping off my sweater for relief, I felt the cycle restart again and again and AGAIN. I did my best version of self-talk. I was brave. I was determined. I ignored my discomfort with the hope that my body would adjust. I have had babies. I have been an athlete. I am strong, and I can fight these nonsensical urges. No amount of internal pep talks and resolve would alter the outcome. The sweater dance continued. My inner dialog only added misery and dripping makeup to the monotony. Make no mistake. Menopause is the master of the body.

Menopause also derails the mind. I had a functioning brain yet forgot details at awkward moments. Despite mastering new technology at work and recalling my shopping list, I couldn't depend upon myself. Forgetfulness was annoying, like pesky ants creeping into the picnic of life. For example, I was driving the car and realized that I didn't know where I was going. I was on the San Mateo bridge if I was lucky, because it gave me time to think. The bridge crosses the lower section of the San Francisco bay and there are no exits until you reach the other side, which takes ten to twenty minutes, depending upon the traffic. Since there was no need for an immediate decision, I could run through all possible destinations. Given enough time, I could assemble my schedule to determine where I intended to go before I had to exit. Sheepishly, I must admit that, more than once, I found myself following a long-abandoned carpool route when I intended to go to my office.

Occasionally, my mind went blank at a most inopportune time. I worked at a company that provided internet technology equipment. One morning I sent an "all hands" message to local employees. The phone system allowed me to dial a code and send a message to everyone. It had one unfortunate glitch. Whatever I recorded went out LIVE. I could not erase and re-record. I picked up the phone and announced my name, "This is Carole..." Then my mind went blank. I had no cohesive thought. I stared at the telephone numbly and mumbled something about a "blonde moment." My company-wide broadcast was a sensation. I wanted to hide, but the message was out. I found my notes and made another call with my intended message. Fortunately, I worked with people who took it in stride. I received only smiles and lighthearted jabs. Please take note: *it is good to work with fun and supportive people when going through menopause. You have no idea what surprises may arise.*

Your experience of menopause will be your own. No doubt you have, or will have, your stories to share. These personal experiences bring us together as women.

Your Story About Aging

Let's get serious for a moment. Menopause or THE CHANGE is one sign that we are aging. It is a clear, physical reminder that we are reaching the middle of our life. Child-bearing is a thing of the past. Your body "shifts." Over time, your height shrinks, and your belly expands. Do you fight these changes? Do you give up the battle, eat what you want, and move into tent-like tops? What does "aging" mean to you? How old is OLD? Our society isn't kind to women "of a certain age." We learn to camouflage birthdays with creams that "minimize the look of fine lines and wrinkles."

Beauty changes. When I was a teenager, I noticed my pimples and awkwardness. I did my best to camouflage my figure flaws. I did not feel beautiful. Now, as I pass the local high school, I see the innate, undeniable beauty of every young woman. Regardless of their size, or nationality, or personality, each girl exudes a universal radiance.

Age changes our expression of beauty. Post-menopausal women are also beautiful, but it is different. We may not have the bloom of youth. Yet, we wear the glow of wisdom that is ageless, classic, warm, and inviting. THE CHANGE is confrontational. While you have been changing every day of your life, suddenly menopause flashes a warning:

- You have a limited lifespan – and a good percentage of it has passed.
- Your body is aging.
- If you have children, they are adults or soon will be.
- If you have parents, they may need your help soon.
- Your life will never be the same.
- What you do now impacts your FUTURE and your FINANCES.

Are you willing to look deeply into yourself to create a conscious and intentional future?

As I went through my self-examination, I was self-conscious. You would think that at mid-life, I would have a better understanding of how to manage money. I made classic mistakes that textbooks warn you to avoid. I was so embarrassed that I made it my mission to study and improve my money management skills. While spending time with experts, I learned to identify risks and understand guarantees. With planning and conscious decisions, you can minimize money problems. I listened to clients who had questions about money. Although everyone wants to control their finances, many find that money has a life of its own. Imagine saving for years, anticipating a solid foundation for retirement. Then in a single week, the market shrinks by half, and retirement is in question. Or you planned to cash in on real estate investments, but in 2009, you found yourself in foreclosure instead.

Your first step on the path to having a healthy view of money is to ask yourself an honest question: how does your heart feel about money? The second step is to vision and daydream. What do you envision in the second half of your life? Are there dreams you left behind? Could a new lifestyle be calling? What if the past no longer held you captive? Could you permit yourself to take a unique road? Or would you make a conscious choice to stay where you are? Your life is up to you.

Now you can devote some time to understand your millionaire choices better. How will you obtain and use the million dollars you need for the rest of your life? Spend time reviewing your financial options: real estate, the market, retirement pensions, 401K, insurance, long-term care expenses, and annuities. While it is futile to provide a single analysis to guide your future investments, you can investigate your options when you know where to look. There are no guarantees, but it does help the spirit and the heart to feel comfortable with your choices.

At the end of each chapter, there are resources to guide you in your self-exploration. Take time to ask questions on the Menopause Millionaire Facebook page. I have learned that the wisest approach to life is to seek the counsel of various people. Listen to what they have to say. Then make up your mind. This life IS, after all, your very own adventure!

Keys For Reflection:
Self-Guided Financial Analysis

Begin by choosing either one or two notebooks to capture your thoughts and emotions. Writing by hand captures your feelings better than an electronic document. No matter how much or how little money you have, it is YOUR FEELING about money that provides prosperity in the last half of your life.

The first section is for observations and feelings. I have always made discoveries about myself through a stream of consciousness approach. Removing any emotional filters and writing whatever comes to mind can produce enlightening results. Write with any technique that appeals to you. If you remember a childhood passion, write it down. If you have a bucket list of adventures to experience in this lifetime, capture it here. Record your wishes and your fears. Let it flow. You need not share this with anyone. A deep dive into consciousness opens up your inner voice. Writing can open the door to your soul. I have often re-read my journal and find surprises that give me clarity.

The second notebook is for your financial history, details, and possibilities for the future. You may share these details with financial professionals and the people who are part of your future. It might be valuable for your spouse or children. Keeping this section distinct from your emotional observations ensures that your thoughts remain private.

Collect the details of what you already own. You may have an accountant or financial software to provide you with a financial statement and record your assets and liabilities.

Assets

Assets consist of everything you own. Your home, cars, clothing, jewelry, and all your possessions are assets. The dollar amount to record is what they are worth **today** if you were selling them. Often your assets are worth less than you think.

You could visit a local estate sale to get a more accurate estimate of what your used "stuff" is worth. Recently, I browsed a local sale and found a desk identical to one I bought many years ago for $2,400. The sales price was $250. I still love my desk, but I won't get rich by selling it. I did discover that estate sales are a great way to make my home more enjoyable without spending much money.

Your home can be a significant asset, and there are several ways to determine the value. If you know a friendly local realtor, they can give you a ballpark estimate based upon values in your neighborhood. If you are selling your home, research local comps and make detailed comparisons. For your Net Worth calculations, you only need a rough estimate. You might also do online research at Zillow.com or Realtor.com. Look for local homes with similar square footage and lot size. Find several homes with comparable kitchens & bathrooms to get an idea of your home's value. Record a value or range of value in your notebook.

If you have made loans to others and are expecting repayment, these are also considered assets. Even if they are loans to your children or parents, include them as assets unless you plan to forgive them, making them a "gift" rather than a loan.

Finally, add your investment funds, retirement funds, 401K, Roth IRA, investment property, pension funds, rental homes, and any other stores of value to your asset column. If you are expecting an inheritance, you might add that to your asset column as well. While future income is NOT acceptable on a standard net worth statement, it is relevant to your financial future. This document is for your planning information only. You do not have to follow strict rules of accounting.

Debt

Debt includes everything you owe. List every debt. Include your mortgage, credit cards, car loans, student loans, and personal loans from friends or family members. If you have co-signed for your child's student loans, include this as debt. (Until paid, it is your debt – even if your child makes all the payments.)

You may have an accountant or accounting software provide you with a financial statement. This document should give you an overview of your assets and liabilities. You will want to know how much value you have accumulated and how much debt you have. Once you have both your assets and debts accounted for, you can determine your net worth.

Assets Minus Debt = NET WORTH

Where Are You Now?

Once you have assembled lists of your assets or items of value and liabilities or debts, you follow the formula above to calculate your net worth. Net worth is a number that you want to track on a regular, perhaps monthly, basis.

Your income increases your net worth while your bills reduce it. Tracking your net worth gives you a good idea of how you are doing with money math. If this kind of tracking is a new habit, can you see how it might be helpful to you? Tracking your net worth brings consciousness to your habits and gives you more opportunities to build the bigger picture of money. An increasing number of online financial programs are available to help track your economic life.

Your Business

Many small business owners integrate home and business expenses. They shift costs to the business to minimize taxes. The company might own their car and pay for repairs and fuel. This practice is acceptable for tax purposes with detailed records for business and personal mileage. Decisions within your company have a significant impact on your future. When calculating your personal net worth, include an asset value for your business. Consider what the business would be worth if you sold it today.

If you don't plan to retire for ten or more years, you can brainstorm ideas to increase the value of your business. If you are a solopreneur, you might research ways to improve the sales value of your business or generate passive income. Do you have a succession plan that supports you in the second half of your life? How does your business contribute to your retirement or vision of the future? Business owners who think ahead can benefit financially. Failing to plan is a recipe for loss of potential value.

You deserve a vibrant and fulfilling life adventure. Continue to imagine your heart-filling experience as we explore the energy of money.

KEYS FOR REFLECTION:

1. Your ideas of value shift over time. To understand your history, review some financial documents from the past. Look at tax returns or Quicken files from more than five years ago. What do you notice about

your income? Your expenses? How do they reflect the
values you had at that time? What has changed now?

2. How do you feel about the way you spend money?
3. Which purchases light you up years later?
4. Which purchases feel like a waste of time and money?
5. What do you learn about yourself as you examine
   your cash flow?

Chapter Three

SCHOOL OF HARD KNOCKS

"Life is an adventure...make it a great one."
~Carole Hodges

I AM NOT a typical money expert or health and aging expert. I am neither a multi-millionaire nor a famous actress. I am an average woman, reaching mid-life and asking, "What is life all about?"

I have learned that experts don't have all the answers. Authentic solutions are within us. Proof that you are on track is in your own heart. You will choose in perfect timing when the opinion of others is no longer a distracting detour from your deliberate course. While life has no guarantees, you can embrace curiosity, exploring life while openly wondering how it will all turn out. The key to life is your own. You can RELAX once you adopt the belief that life is your unique adventure. You call the shots and set the targets. We share our life with others, knowing that each person is a fellow adventurer. We know that we will have triumph and defeat, love and loss, challenge, learning, and surprise. A day comes when you experience your greatest fear, then find with astonishment that life continues, flowers bloom, and the sun rises. Or you reach the ultimate experience of joy, profound as an Olympic medal in your human adventure. You thought you would be completely satisfied before discovering with amazement that you want MORE! Life contains both the joyful heights and the seemingly bottomless depths.

Early in my life, I felt blessed. As the eldest of six children, my parents expected me to lead by example. I did well in school, received a partial scholarship in college, and had the unique experience of being the homecoming queen in high school and college. I graduated from college in three years and got married before my graduation at age twenty. I was in a hurry to grow up.

By the time I reached my thirties, my life appeared smooth on the outside. I had three beautiful children, a lovely home, and volunteered for my church and community. One day a member of my church gave me his observations. He uttered words I have never forgotten, "Life will bring you only velvet bumps." The gentleman who said this was the husband of a friend. From his perspective, I had life all figured out. He intended to compliment me. I could always make things "look" good. Yet underneath the external wrapper was a bumpy reality. By my mid-forties, I found sharp rocks and boulders replacing those "velvet bumps." Life became unmanageable.

My young children were the bright lights in my world. My son and two daughters each demonstrated particular talents that set them apart. Each is intelligent, likable, and full of fun and energy. I cherish them.

One day, friends introduced me to dance classes which filled my inner need for expression. I began with ballet before adding jazz and tap classes. I was willing to suffer through the discipline of learning the basics and the pull of sore muscles unaccustomed to such demands. Dancing also opened an opportunity to perform in community theatre. Theatre was magic, a fantasy world of joy and community. I could burst into song and dance at the downbeat of the orchestra.

However, the foundation of this vision was rarely joyful. I was in business with my husband, and the company was failing. By the time I was 46, I had taken temporary office work to provide money for groceries. We stopped making our mortgage and car payments. Creditors bombarded our phones asking for money. Process servers pounded at our front door to deliver legal demands. We did what seemed logical at the time: we didn't answer the doorbell. Even our children learned to ignore the doorbell and the knocking on the door. The entire family pretended that we weren't home as our lives descended into chaos. Life slid from a pretense of normalcy into the deranged.

My marriage slowly disintegrated over the years. Like an old house that wasn't tended or repaired, the foundation of our relationship had crumbled. Any honest and heartfelt communication, which is the glue that maintains a connection, vanished years before. We did not speak as our family world crumbled. Our home was a sad place to be. Money vanished. I found it too painful to address the many underlying issues. I couldn't see a solution, and we had no plan to move forward.

Our oldest daughter, Corinne, was 25. She returned to live

at home after graduating from college. Corinne had a passion for dance. She was a multi-talented high achiever. As a young child, my daughter was an excellent gymnast, soccer player, and swimmer. Then at age twelve, she began taking ballet and jazz, which quickly won her heart. She dropped her other sports to focus on dance.

Corinne developed into an exceptional dancer who loved new challenges. She was also a brilliant student, and multiple colleges accepted her. She was drawn to New York University (NYU) because it was close to many prominent dance companies. She received a partial scholarship, and at the time she started school, we were in a financial position where we felt we could squeeze her tuition into the budget. Before she completed her studies, our finances changed, and she acquired significant student debt. Corinne graduated from NYU with summa cum laude honors. Her dance talents had also landed an understudy position with the Merce Cunningham dance company.

However, Corinne had a dark side. In her early teens, she alternated between high moments of bliss and lower bouts of despair. Corinne was bipolar. After graduation from NYU, she was penniless and unable to hold a job, so she moved home from New York. Once home, she made daily announcements that she would kill herself if we couldn't give her money or the car.

I felt helpless. I followed the routines of daily living while my mind circled endlessly, looking for solutions that never came. Our business was failing. I jumped at any temp jobs I could find while looking for permanent work. What little I earned bought necessities. Although I couldn't afford the recommended twice-weekly sessions, I located a psychiatrist who could work with Corinne monthly.

Mental illness is a curse. Television might have you believe that depression is a passing illness cured with a pill. The truth is that mental illness can overcome both the individual and their family. In Corinne's delusional mind, she was fine. She wanted the world around her to change. The psychiatrist prescribed anti-depressants which would temporarily normalize her state of mind. Yet, she hated medication because it took away her natural "high" from dancing. I juggled her demands with the family requirements. Some days she dropped me off at my job so she could use the vehicle. Some days I needed the car, and I held my breath, hoping for the best.

Her threats were a daily ritual. At any time, I could have called mental health authorities to have her held for psychological evaluation. I discussed this possibility with her psychiatrist. It was not a long-term solution. Hospitals could only keep her for 72 hours to get her medicated. After 72 hours, the patient is sent home until the next time. Mental illness is insidious. Even the brightest and most talented people can be afflicted. It is a parent's worst nightmare.

I felt like I was on the ocean with a rowboat and one paddle. No matter what I did, I could not see the shore. My only choice was to paddle and hope for the best. I wanted to do the right thing without any inkling of what was right. I questioned myself daily: "What else can I do?" "How can I pay the bills?" "What can I do to help Corinne?" I never found the answer.

One late afternoon, I opened the door to Corinne's room to tell her I was leaving for a few minutes to pick up her sister at the train station. She was speaking to a friend on the phone and waved to me. I was gone about 20 minutes. When I returned, her sister went into the kitchen. Then I heard her yelling, "Corinne hung herself!"

The words hung in the air. My world went dim as I moved into crisis mode. I ran toward the kitchen. Corinne was hanging by a dog leash from a balcony railing outside the kitchen window. I ran outside to stand below her while her sister ran upstairs with a knife to cut the leash. We had her down quickly, and I caught her below. Her sister called 911. An ambulance was on the way. When they arrived, Corinne was still breathing and they rushed her to the hospital.

Miraculously, Corinne lived for three days. However, she never regained consciousness. On the third day, she developed pneumonia. There was little hope. Our fragile family sat in a small private room at the hospital to speak with the doctor. Together we agreed to stop life support. Extended family members had flown into town as emotional support. Almost a dozen friends and family in Corinne's hospital room share remembrances and offered hope and prayers.

As several people prepared to leave, we looked at Corinne. She had stopped breathing. Her spirit had left us. I was numb. The sky turned grey. I had a deep sense of helplessness. Despite her warning threats, we could not escape the inevitable end. Life felt empty in the face of death. Friends delivered food. Without their generosity, I would not have eaten. Our family pulled apart, never to be the same. Grief encompassed each of us, and words were meaningless.

The chaos of our life didn't stop. The assaults of creditors continued as they bombarded us with calls day after day. I answered a call from Bank of America about an overdue credit card payment. I told the nameless woman on the phone that my daughter died. The woman on the telephone droned on without emotion, "Your credit will be impaired if we don't receive your payment by tomorrow." The absurdity of her message hit me in the gut. I blurted out, "Some things are more important than my credit!" and slammed down the phone.

I needed a real job. A supportive recruiter helped me through the process. She kept my circumstances to herself, not sharing with prospective employers. Two weeks after Corinne's funeral, I took a position as a sales assistant in technology. It wasn't a challenging job. I learned the technology of video conferencing but wasn't under stress. I showed up every day to work. I smiled and said nothing about my home life. I was fearful that they would never hire me if anyone knew my reality, and I needed that job.

Corinne died on August 23. Less than six months later, in January, we declared corporate and personal bankruptcy. The following May, I saved enough for an apartment and moved out. Nothing could revive my lifeless marriage. Our divorce was final in September.

In a single year, I lost a daughter, declared bankruptcy, and divorced. Sadly, even this narrative is missing many details. The pain and suffering of my remaining two children seared my heart. My love was not enough to shield them from the storm of confusion and heartbreak. Confronting my limitations, I surrendered and embraced humility. I cannot solve a host of problems, but that will never stop me from striving to make life better. Perhaps none of us have a life of "velvet bumps." We awaken our inner strength when confronted by challenges that shake our world view, and become strong by facing the impossible, surrounded by fear but with a firm focus on hope.

I looked for comfort in simple things throughout those turbulent times. As my brain circled aimlessly, I wanted to stop the madness. I sought out authentic moments hidden in plain sight. I stopped at a lush park and felt the green blades of freshly mowed grass flex beneath me as I lay on the ground, surrounded by the fresh scent. I was captivated by the divine pattern of nature in a single leaf as nature's symmetry filled my imagination and senses. The magnificence of a flower offers peace to a troubled soul.

I sought out dandelions going to seed and ready to release their white floating webs. As a child, I learned to make a wish and send magic floaties airborne. In seconds, a flurry of wishes wafted away. In these moments, I escaped my pain, sprouting hope that God and spirit had a higher plan. I had to trust and believe what I could not yet see. In those moments, I sensed a higher truth. If God or a universal spirit created such complex and unexpected beauty all around for our enjoyment, that same spirit would provide for me. Love and faith became my foundation for living.

I know that you have had your share of challenges. You don't reach the middle of life without education from your own "hard knocks." I have spoken to women who have lost a husband or struggled to fight disease. Others have had abusive spouses. One woman and her son lived in her car as her only shelter until she could find a job. Another successful woman lost her entire retirement savings by trusting them to a CPA who defrauded her. Both had to deal with the betrayal of their trust. Your story is your own.

Human life is your adventure. You might be a jungle explorer or a superhero. Notice what arose for you as you read my story. Stop to acknowledge the trials you have survived. Your challenges may be in the past, or you may be fighting them today. You have endured disappointments and disasters. What inner strengths allowed you to take the next step? You never stopped, and now you are here. You have earned the right to step into wisdom.

Honor the challenges you confront today. When you celebrate your truth, you continue to grow. Pay attention to feelings in your gut, your pelvis, your heart, and your head. Your body is a tuning fork that resonates with your inner truth. If you are experiencing pain or fear, be kind to yourself. Look for a slice of nature to calm you. A single plant or pet can heal when you bring yourself to be fully present. Corral your wandering mind and observe details around you. Appreciate beauty, scents, and sounds. Allow nature and spirit to support you and release your illusion of control. Honor the strength that is YOU. Wherever you have been, whatever you have experienced, you are here. Pull the inner strength of steel from the fires of your experience. Pat yourself on the back because you are a winner. You made it to TODAY!

Mid-life is the time to celebrate the woman you have become. You have many more opportunities to grow and learn. Each choice may open fresh experiences and send you on a novel trajectory. Keep on growing!

KEYS FOR REFLECTION:

Take a few moments to answer each of the questions below. Consider how you have changed over the years.

1. What challenges have you faced?
2. How have your challenges impacted your view of life?
3. How do you find inner strength when faced with problems?

Chapter Four

YOUR COMING OF AGE

"There is a fountain of youth: it is your mind, your talents, the creativity you bring to your life and the lives of people you love. When you learn to tap this source, you will truly have defeated age."

~Sophia Loren

HOW OLD DO YOU FEEL? Or maybe I should ask, "How old do you feel when you DON'T look in the mirror?" After age 70, my mother often said she was shocked when she looked in the mirror and saw wrinkles and white hair. She had a memory of the slim figure and the raven black hair of her youth. Mom often said that she continued to feel like a curious teenager inside. She was a lifelong explorer. Her innate curiosity was alive and well, even as a few aches and pains slowed her pace. Was mom practicing self-deception? Or did she have a secret to boosting her vitality? Age can wrinkle the skin and diminish one's energy. But what about inner spirit? How does your SOUL deal with aging?

At mid-life, an unanswered question pleads for an answer. The soul wants to know, "Why am I here?" I have longed for a flash of white light in the evening sky accompanied by a massive voice booming a definitive answer. As years glide past, I would gladly accept a whispered response or a calm affirming tap on my shoulder. I envy those that have found and followed their vision. I continue to question my life's purpose while fearing that I may be the "odd duck" who can't find my obvious purpose while others follow their divine guidance.

I have been called an "old soul." I used to think it was a compliment that affirmed an accumulation of hard-won wisdom. Then I heard a talk on YouTube by the late Dolores Cannon. Dolores was known as a hypnotherapist who specialized in past life regression. In sessions with her clients, she accumulated extensive documentation about otherworldly connections. Through the stories of others' experiences, she gathered exciting observations of life beyond this human experience.

Dolores said that an "old soul" is one who had returned multiple times to the human experience because they failed to decipher their life purpose on their first journey. The "old soul" must return again and again until accomplishing its mission. This possibility humbles me. As an "old soul," I am open and willing to learn this life game. Longevity alone does not guarantee wisdom. How might we live a fulfilling second half of life that expands our soul and makes the entire journey worthwhile? Let's consider our lives as experiences of our own making.

Outrageous Choice

Years ago, I had a coaching business named "Outrageous Choice." One of my foundational beliefs is that each of us creates our lives via our choices. We choose what to wear and eat, where to work or play, with whom we spend time, and what to read, watch, or do from morning to night. Each of these choices sculpts our human experience. You are the creator of your life. If you live by this model of self-choice, then "success" is a label that you award to yourself. Sadly, many people follow someone else's model, taking the higher paying job rather than one which inspired them. The advice of a parent, best friend, or spouse could lead away from inner wisdom. Making choices might not be straightforward, yet choices define your life.

When I was marketing "Outrageous Choice," I frequently went to networking events. After introducing myself, I would ask someone, "What is YOUR outrageous choice?" My question prompted fascinating discussions. People would share childhood dreams or a goal of success beyond their current reality. I observed an instant change in expression as they considered an "outrageous choice." Their energy expanded, and smiles lit up each face as they imagined the life they had either forgotten or stopped believing. I felt as though I had a magic wand that awakened hope and opportunity.

What is your outrageous choice? Rediscovering your unexplored dreams and visions is the first step to creating their reality. When you feel inspired by an "outrageous choice," STOP! Put down this book and let your imagination fly! Start writing in your journal, including all details. Let your spirit expand. You are not making commitments, nor are you creating a business plan. You are mapping a vision of your soul's landscape. You could pick up a pen or crayon to draw designs or pictures instead of capturing words. Express your outrageous choices however they come to you. You could even start singing or dancing!

Have you ever experienced a scene in a movie that captured your imagination? Perhaps a frustrated executive took refuge in the country and throws open the shutters to a lush landscape of rolling hills. Or you feel the wind in your hair when you see Supergirl fly. Moments of unexpected ecstasy are clues.

In my imagination, I see the Live Aid audience rocking out with Freddy Mercury to "Bohemian Rhapsody." I long to be on that stage with energetic vibrations pulsing through my veins, uplifting thousands who connect with love and joy. My idea may be crazy in this life. I want to be a rock star! But why not ask, "How can I create such an experience?" Can I energize crowds to experience love and joy while embracing their best selves? How can we stretch beyond the impossible? I'm getting ideas even as I write.

Be willing to acknowledge your unique heart vibes, looking for new or hidden possibilities. Notice what speaks to your heart. Can you open the door to inner courage? What might happen if you stepped outside your expectations? How long have you ignored or postponed your dreams for your family? Or to support your spouse? Were you ever afraid to put your heart's desire into words? You have the second half of life ahead of you. Consider what you need to make hidden dreams your new reality. Now is the time to believe what is possible. Your legacy is what you create from this point forward. You can share it or hide it behind wrinkles and weak bones. But ONLY YOU can decide for yourself.

Aging

Aging is NOT the same for everyone. REAL changes happen, which shift your worldview beyond laughter or despair, procrastination, or ostrich-like denial. Change is neither good nor bad. It is inevitable. Your attitude and actions will determine whether you transform into the wise goddess, or whether you start the process of withering into a white-haired old lady, resenting every minute.

I encourage you to explore your dreams as long as you are alive. You need not shelve plans prematurely. Yet you are maturing. Aging can be harsh. The changes that happen over a few years can often be EXTREME. Notice how women vary from their 60's, 70's, 80's and 90's. Some women let age define them, but not all. How do you view aging? Can you still make news at age 90? Ruth Bader Ginsberg served on the Supreme Court of the United States until her death at age 87. Despite repeated bouts with cancer, she returned to work until she left this world. RBG was a woman of grace and power who left her stamp on the law and life of America. She continued to see herself as vital her entire life.

Is there a magic potion for vitality as we age? Let me introduce you to Phyllis Sues, who wrote a blog in the Huffington Post (*Phyllis Sues "Celebrating Being Here at 92" Huff Post, April 3, 2015*) about how she felt as she celebrated her 92nd birthday. Phyllis Sues is now 98 and still enjoying life. Phyllis states her philosophy simply:

"To look good and feel good is work. To look great and feel great is a full-time job. There is no cheating! It's daily! Minute-by-minute, second-by-second. This is the process I love and love to work on. The reward is liking myself and living a creative life. I will turn 90 on April 4 and hope I can still create this in 10 years. I started my first fashion label at 50, became a musician and learned Italian and French in my 70s, took tango and trapeze at 80, and walked into my first yoga class at 85. So, if you think you're old, think again!"

Phyllis is an inspiration. She decides her future and renews that decision each day. Consider your own life. What decisions are YOU making? What choices must you make to be healthy 10, 20, or 30 years from now? Do you have a plan to learn new skills? Why not start a new career? What do you need to explore and expand your possibilities? Have you permitted yourself to live fully?

"Step out of the history that is holding you back. Step into the new story you are willing to create."
~Oprah Winfrey

What story are you creating? Here are the elements to consider:

- *YOUR BODY*. Your body is your responsibility for as long as you live. Our bodies impact our confidence and freedom every day. While it is possible to push our physical limits and ignore our bodies when we are young, it is now time to examine how our choices impact our health. Vitality and health give us the foundation for other choices.

- **RELATIONSHIPS.** Who are the people that surround you? Do you love and admire them or recognize that they are deflating and robbing you of energy? How did they get into your world? Are they relatives, neighbors, or co-workers? If you lined them up and considered their impact on you, which ones would you keep in your life? Which relationships promote mutual love and support? Which relationships encourage your growth? Which relationships uplift and energize you? Are there toxic behaviors that you wish to eliminate? Which relationships do you cherish? How do you contribute to other people? Why or why not? Life is never static. Permit yourself to have the relationships that you want!

- **MONEY.** As we move into the second half of life, money can determine what is available to us. Stop to identify ongoing income sources. How much social security will you receive? How much have you saved or invested? Will you receive an inheritance from your parents? Can you rely on support from your children, friends, or family? Personal financial health puts a frame around the picture of our lives, even determining where we live and our activities. Economic focus is not new, but our choices at this time of life are critical. The monetary foundation you build at 50 becomes your future. If you do not create a foundation today, your options begin to disappear. The miracle of compound interest requires many years to bloom. Be honest with yourself. Will you have enough to retire? Even a million dollars will only allow you $4-8,000 per month in retirement. Now is your time to evaluate your future. Money is a priority. What you choose from this moment has real-life consequences.

- **VALUES & PASSIONS.** What is that special spice that gives you identity and meaning? What makes you feel like a rock star? How do you want to care for others? You have the secret sauce that you have been developing over the years. Consider what brings out the very best in you.

- What is the role of family in your life? Do you intend to live close to your children or parents? You are moving away from the busy world of motherhood. As your children reach adulthood, a relationship reset is healthy. You might find joy in becoming a grandmother, or maybe not. The decision is not yours. Your children will create their own families and life paths. You can love them whether they are near or even if they separate their life from you. Be your best, no matter what happens.

- How deep is your spiritual life? Are you part of a church? Or part of a community that cares for each other? What connects you to a power that is greater than our human life? People who feel secure in their beliefs frequently handle stress and adversity with more ease.

- Are there causes that ignite you? Whether you lead a political march through town or care for others quietly and without acknowledgment, you are making an impact. As other family and career obligations lighten, you might become a fundraiser for abandoned animals. Or you could bring food to seniors who can't get out. What are the causes that light you up?

- What makes you feel ALIVE? Passion can be subtle energy. When you are involved in something you love, time melts away as creativity flows through you. Passion arises at times of profound joy as well as times of anger. One day you may announce, *"I'm not gonna take this anymore."* You are experiencing passion. It gets you out of your seat and into action. Or you may feel like falling in love with life.

- The day will arrive when you may leave your job or career behind. What will be next?

Menopause is a time to rediscover your identity. Remember when you were a teenager, creating your identity? You asked yourself, "Who am I? What will I wear? Who will I hang out with?" Menopause mirrors adolescence. You have another opportunity to explore who you are. What is important now? Who do I want to be? Now is not the time to decide you are OLD. Instead, it is a time of conscious choice.

KEYS FOR REFLECTION:

Label a section of your journal "Outrageous Choice." Write out your thoughts on your dreams and visions. Come back to this section as new thoughts show up. Let yourself be open and flow. Your journal is only for you. Sharing is optional. Save it for those who will support you in creating this new vision.

Chapter Five

YOUR BODY AT MENOPAUSE

"You can free yourself from aging by reinterpreting your body and by grasping the link between belief and biology."
~Deepak Chopra

AS MENOPAUSE ENTERED MY LIFE, the comparison with adolescence was inescapable. My body, having carried me through all life's adventures, was changing. Remember that strange teenage feeling as your breasts began to sprout? I had similar strange feelings as they began to expand and relax. (On a bad day, I might say they drooped.)

Changes in the body at menopause may be subtle or extreme. One day you notice that your periods have disappeared. Or you may wake up in the morning wondering what demon has taken over your internal thermometer and distorted your mirror.

The inescapable truth is that things will never be the same again. YOU will never be the same again. You may find yourself looking at the latest "wrinkle erasing" potion or considering laser treatments to revive the youthful energy in your face. Lotions and potions can boost the ego, helping you feel better about the aging process. But they are not a panacea.

Your body is sending you messages that encourage you to take an honest look at your lifestyle. Your habits are reflected in your vitality and experience today. And here is the good news. Health problems are NOT an inescapable part of aging. You could have another 50 years or more on this planet. Now is the time to make healthful choices with a long-term perspective. You may already have noticed that you find it more challenging to bounce back after a binge than it was 20 years ago. Whether your binge is ice cream or alcohol, you wear the consequences. What support do you need to follow a healthy diet plan with regular exercise? Your enjoyment of life, your resilience to disease, and the size of your bank account depend upon your health choices.

Perhaps your busy schedule prevents you from a focus on your health. You may be managing your career to save for a comfortable retirement. While this excuse could have a grain of truth, your body will never buy it. You aren't a kid anymore. Your incredible body has brought you through decades of growth, but now exercise and healthy food are mandatory. Subtle reminders, like tiredness or indigestion, take center stage. These minor aggravations can quickly escalate into pain or disease if you continue to ignore your body's cries for health help.

At mid-life, attention to your health is often more crucial than your finances. Poor health robs you of enjoyment of life AND depletes your savings faster than any other expense. Too often, I meet clients who decide to get life insurance or long-term care insurance to bolster their retirement security, only to be declined because of health problems. When you have health issues, your choices shrink. Health insurance does not cover all expenses. Medicare is not free. Surgery to replace hips or fix backs is costly. Co-pays for some drug prescriptions have a monthly cost which is more than a new car payment. Medical care for your body is rarely optional. Taking care of your health is a SMART FINANCIAL MOVE. You might eliminate more than $100,000 of medical expense by taking time to eat healthy meals and take walks. Think of this as an opportunity to get paid for doing something that feels good. Would you be more likely to take a walk if you were getting $50 per hour?

Here is a simple formula to give you more energy and protect a chunk of your retirement funds. If you have medical restrictions, check with your doctor for approval. Your objective is to get moving as much as you can. Check with friends or professionals to support you as you develop new habits that you can follow for the rest of your life. Select actions that belong on your priority list every single week:

- Exercise a minimum of 3 times a week. You can start small and increase every month.
- Begin with 3 to 20-minute walks if you are inactive.
- Find classes with friends to keep you motivated.
- Look for hobbies that get you moving. Tennis, hiking, skiing, yoga, dance can all be the beginning of a healthy body.
- Gradually increase your workouts until you are regularly doing 3-5 hours of exercise weekly

Listen to Your Body

You need to nourish your body in new ways. As we age, our nutrition needs change. Some doctors are more aware of these changes than others. Do your homework when you choose a doctor. Often, general nutrition recommendations list only the minimal and average requirements. Blood work will reveal how you compare to these averages. Some doctors only discuss your results if they are abnormal. Ideally, you want to have more specific nutrition targets which lead to optimal health. Ask your doctor for specific recommendations for your age and physical condition.

Make a list of any issues you want to address, such as weight, junk food addictions, excessive alcohol, or other substance abuse. Before you are ready to make a change, you must be conscious of your habits and how they will impact your future. You alone must take care of your body. You don't need to make yourself feel bad. I don't believe in "fat-shaming" or other negative emotions that people use to punish themselves. However, your body is integral to your life experience, and YOU are the only one in control. If you have a healthy life vision as you age, you can use positive goals to keep you on track.

Your body will also give you clues. Pay attention to nature's red flags. When I was in my late forties, I suddenly developed an aversion to fried food. My first incident was a wave of nausea after eating McDonald's fries. I thought it was a fluke until it happened a second time. Nausea also hit me after eating Colonel Sanders crispy fried chicken and again after eating a plate of fish and chips.

My body delivered a clear message that fried food was NOT

for me. Friends may suggest that you take a pill and keep eating whatever you want. Be conscious of your choices. When you add prescriptions rather than changing your behavior, you will miss out on the message your body is sending. Once you understand that food fried in grease can usher in diabetes and nasty liver problems, you may prefer to listen to your body's wise message and make prompt adjustments. Take time to listen; your body is speaking the truth for you.

How to Change a Habit

Food cravings demonstrate the emotional nature of preferences. You want certain foods and dislike others because of prior experience. However, many people continue to eat foods that cause them discomfort and destroy their health. You have a choice. I learned to retrain my desire naturally using a systematic process which I am sharing below.

NLP (Neuro-Linguistic Programming) is the study of how we think and store words and experience. By understanding our learned emotional connections with foods, we can change habits that do not serve us. I used my physical response to fried food to change my behavior with ease. My experience of discomfort strengthened my willpower. This technique uses self-hypnosis to make lasting changes. You begin by making a firm decision to change. No one can make this decision for you. Convinced this will not work? You can be right by simply deciding that it will not work. However, when you decide that your life and health will improve quickly when you change the foods you eat, you will be thrilled to use a tool to eliminate foods that do not serve you. Your body will work with you to support this healthy shift. Follow these steps, which allowed me to eliminate fried food, doughnuts, and sugary cakes from my diet for all time. I no longer suffer from stomach upset, and I do not miss out on good foods. Here are the simple steps:

First: Be aware of your response to food. When you recognize that a specific food upsets you, take notice of the discomfort. Ask yourself if you are willing to eliminate this food to enjoy good health and self-support. You need to make this decision before proceeding.

Second: Memorize the uncomfortable or nauseous feeling from eating a specific food. Feel the discomfort within your body. Amplify how bad it feels. Remember how horrible you felt. Imagine eating or drinking that food and feeling nauseous. Feel any additional negative responses, like itchy skin, watery eyes, sneezing, or choking.

Third: The next time you see that unhealthy food, step into that feeling of discomfort. Amplify the greasiness and sugary overwhelm or other attributes as you remember how badly you felt when you ate it. At the same time, repeat to yourself how grateful you are that you never need to eat this food again. Revive this negative emotion every time you see this food. LOCK-IN the negative feeling of nausea. Acknowledge your pain and discomfort as you look at the food that caused it. Mentally taste the food while acknowledging that it never really tasted good. Vow to remember how bad you feel whenever you look at that food in the future.

By following this method, you are setting a powerful anchor for yourself. The next time you see fried food, cake, or whatever you choose to eliminate, you can activate your anchor. REMEMBER THE FEELING of nausea that you get from that food. Remember how awful you felt. Do you want to feel that bad again?

I have used this method to eliminate fried food and those overly sweet flat birthday cakes from my diet. If forced to put a piece of cake on my plate for social occasions, I find it easy enough to set it aside or offer it to someone else who doesn't yet have a piece. I now feel that specific food is repulsive and easily choose not to eat it. When you listen to your body and respect your health, you can learn to love your healthy body. Even when friends think they will tempt me, it becomes easy to say NO. Instead, I feel good because I have made a conscious choice for my health. Try it yourself!

If you are a parent, you may find this process all too familiar. I had a brother who hated peas. If you made him eat them, he would gag and spit them out. Children attach emotion to food quickly, and you can do this as well. You don't need much training. Just return to your childhood. Decide that a portion of food is repulsive. Tap into your genuine feelings of nausea or headache to confirm how disgusting it is. Whenever you look at it, feel that disgust and nausea. Like a stubborn young child, you will not want to eat it. Test the emotional hook technique to improve your eating habits and serve your ongoing health.

Know What Your Are Eating

What is your knowledge of nutrition? Do you read food labels? Do you buy organic? Do you purchase non-GMO? How do you choose what to eat daily?

When you eat high nutrient ingredients and remove empty calories such as sugar and carbs, you improve your health. You have a head start on a vigorous second half if you are already in tune with good nutrition.

If this is new to you, don't feel bad. Most Americans never learn much about nutrition and fall for the myth that eating nutritious food is expensive. The truth is that ignorance and poor health are devastatingly costly. The price of processed food is often more than organic vegetables and essential nutrition.

I had the good fortune of having a mother who studied to become a doctor before becoming a mom. When I was born, she devoted herself to motherhood and applied her health and nutrition expertise to her family. My mother was allergic to corn products, and any form of corn would give her a migraine headache.

When high fructose corn syrup came on the market, it replaced sugar in all types of products: cereals, ice cream, desserts, and even canned fruit and vegetables. As a result, my mother had more migraine headaches. She was never a person to suffer in silence. The entire family shared her migraine misery. I don't blame her for being cross and irritated, but it wasn't fun.

Mom was also a scientist. She explored the causes of migraines and traced them to her corn allergy. Then she went into action. Not only did she read labels for hidden corn syrup, but she taught her children to read labels. As a result, everyone in our family became more aware of what we eat. We eliminated corn syrup long before medical researchers discovered its destructive effect on the body and overall health.

Our family ban on corn syrup eliminated Twinkies and HoHo's from our home, as well as canned vegetables and a host of other items. I suspect that much of the obesity today could be traced to the introduction of corn syrup as a hidden component in processed foods. It added sweetness which some might say made those foods more "addictive." You had some and wanted more. Wanting more was the marketers' dream that added to sales. The fattening of America came after the addition of corn syrup in the 1970s. By the 1980s, there was a surge in both obesity and diabetes. I found it eye-opening to watch the 50th anniversary of the first moon landing in 1969. There were video shots of people gathering to watch the rocket liftoff. They looked very different from Americans today for a simple reason: None of them were fat! There were Americans of every age and race, and they all looked slim and fit.

In retrospect, my mother's headaches were a gift to our family. Eliminating corn syrup saved us from a host of common diseases. Diabetes soared after introducing high fructose corn syrup, yet we have had no diabetes in my family.

You may not have had a mother like mine. However, if you are NOT a label reader, it is time to start. The first thing to notice is the amount of sugar in foods you buy. An average woman at age 50 should keep her sugar consumption to 25 grams or less per day. Limiting your sugar is relatively easy if you are eating fresh fruits and vegetables. However, processed foods are a different matter. I recently picked up a bottle of ginger beer. I love the taste of ginger, yet the amount of sugar in a single serving was 60 grams. That amount is more than double the 25 grams that I allow myself per day. Another culprit is the "health juices" in many stores. A popular acai drink has 40 grams of sugar in an 8 oz glass. If I choose a boost of this drink, I make it a 2 oz shot and nothing more.

There is an interesting side-effect to minimizing your sugar intake. You may find that you begin to prefer more natural food with less sugar. I find that my body had become an honest guide. When I am out for a meal and not reading a label, over-sugared foods are now unappealing. I do not struggle with the willpower to choose healthy food. I prefer it.

After minimizing sugar, a second health culprit is carbohydrates from white flour. Recent diets that avoid all carbohydrates can be misleading. Vegetables such as broccoli, carrots, and peas have carbohydrates, and some people eliminate them. Unless you have a specific dietary issue, there is no need to avoid these vegetables. However, white flour carbohydrate is a filler. You will find it in crackers and snacks, cookies and bread. Read labels and learn which of your everyday foods have white flour.

Here is another tip. When you look at an ingredient list, each item is listed by weight. In other words, the first ingredient has the highest volume by weight in the finished product. Sugar and flour near the top of the ingredient list are signs of nutritionally empty food.

Over time I have found ways to eliminate most white flour. I like to bake and have learned to use flour alternatives such as almond, oat, coconut, and tapioca flours. However, the results are not always desirable when you make substitutions for white flour without learning the different qualities of alternative flours. I encourage you to seek recipes created for specific flours. I have learned that when I use almond and coconut flour, it does not hold together. I may find a sheet full of cookie crumbs. The addition of some oat or tapioca flour keeps the dough together. I often Google recipes for specific flours and discover many new ideas. Friends request many of my dessert recipes for parties. What's even better is that guests have no idea they are eating low-sugar, low-carb deserts! And alternative flours are available in most stores as well as on Amazon.com.

The Three-Week Nutrition Discovery Plan
The Fortune in Your Food

Here is a simple plan to improve your health and nutrition:

1. Week 1 - Start a food journal

a. Write down what you eat and when you eat it. Do this for a week. Take note of both foods and beverages. Make a note of alcoholic drinks, marijuana, and prescription use of pain relievers, sleeping aids, and anti-depressants. If you use any caffeine energy boosters, note that too.
b. Save the labels on processed foods to be accurate about food content.
c. Notice how you feel at various points during the day, especially:

   i. Upon waking – note how you feel and how you slept
   ii. 10 am
   iii. Noon
   iv. 2 pm
   v. 5 pm
   vi. 8 pm to bedtime

d. At the end of the week, notice any correlations between your food intake, energy, and sleep.

2. WEEK 2 – MAKING HEALTHIER CHOICES

a. Choose one item to change.

b. Look at your use of alcohol or drugs first. If you felt sluggish after a social night, consider a change.

c. One of the most impactful is to minimize white sugar and high fructose sugars from your diet.

d. Stevia is a natural non-sugar sweetener for coffee or tea. It comes from a natural leaf and is not a chemical. It does impact insulin production, and it is best to minimize its use.

e. Coconut sugar is a low glycemic substitute for white sugar in baking.

d. Continue to journal your food and your response to it.

3. WEEK 3 – FIND A SUPPORT SYSTEM WITH FRIENDS or a professional to help you create the life-long path to health through good nutrition. You determine your focus for success.

a. Make it a lifelong habit to take note of what you eat and how you are feeling.

b. Do your food research to optimize your diet.

c. Seek health professionals who focus on "optimal health."

WHAT YOU EAT HAS A CONSIDERABLE IMPACT ON YOUR health. Going back to the words of Phyllis Sues, the value you put on YOU is a day-to-day, moment-to-moment process. You can never take the health of your body for granted. But you can have your optimal health if you START NOW. After three weeks of consciously monitoring your food and exercise, you will begin to change your energy and focus. Best of all, you are treating yourself well. Now is a PERFECT time to improve your health.

If you are married, include your spouse in your eating and exercise plans when feasible. If you get pushback, then do this for yourself. You can share new recipes, and perhaps your spouse will become a fan.

You can also invite some girlfriends to follow the program with you. Ask them for their advice and help. If you have friends who prefer their bad habits, bless them and find others to support you.

Friends help friends. I noticed that a girlfriend could have wine, vodka drinks, and marijuana without a problem but ONLY when she had them on separate nights. Every single time she combined any of these, she had a headache the next day. I brought this to her attention, and she acknowledged the connection. I am neither her mother nor monitor, so her actions are her own. But now, she recognizes her responsibility for how she feels the morning after. Be a friend to others and ask them to provide you with feedback on your habits. We are sometimes blind to solutions that are obvious to our friends.

As you enter another phase of life, take time to appreciate and protect your God-given life. The physical change of menopause is the perfect time to improve your health. YOU

DESERVE a FABULOUS LIFE! Why not look at that woman in the mirror and tell her that she is fabulous? A higher power chose your parents and brought you here to live your best life. It is time to cooperate with spirit and live each day fully. Your good health is worth more than a million. Be rich and delight in feeling good. You DESERVE IT!

KEYS FOR REFLECTION:

1. Review and take action.

    a. Journal your "outrageous choices."
    b. Choose one or more ideas you want to pursue.
    c. Get started!

2. REVIEW IDEAS TO MOVE AND EXERCISE.

    a. Decide on a specific plan and stick to it. Give yourself a daily goal.
    b. If you fall off track, start again the next day.
    c. Give yourself a goal and a reward for making progress.

3. Review your three-week discovery plan.

    a. Journal your observations about food habits.
    b. Begin helpful changes.
    c. Get support from your spouse, friends, and doctor.

4. JUST DO IT!

Chapter Six

RELATION SHIFTS

"It's not what we have in life, but who we have in our life that matters."

~Anonymous

IF LIFE ISN'T juicy enough as your body changes from one moment to the next, you can also expect changes in your relationships. Marriages, parenting, families, and communities are all shifting.

I have always been fascinated by people. When I was only five, I camouflaged myself under a fir tree to observe as people walked past on the sidewalk. I watched and listened to what they said and did. My curiosity has continued my entire life, although I am no longer a peeping tom inside a fir tree. I studied a host of subjects related to human behavior, including communication, psychology, personality styles, and more. None of these studies answered my underlying question, "Why do we need each other?"

Within each human being is a longing for deep connection. Each of us craves love from a spouse, family, or community. We experience moments of fulfillment and deep connection. Then someone pulls away, stealing the warm feelings and leaving behind a blanket of loneliness.

At mid-life, you come face to face with this human longing. Everything shifts as your children grow up, your parents grow old, and new circumstances challenge your marriage. People who are foundational rocks in your existence crumble to sand, and it is easy to lose your emotional footing.

There are three common ways to approach relationship challenges. First, you could decide that you no longer need the human connection. If you choose this path, you find yourself becoming a loner who keeps to herself. Couples sometimes choose this path; "You and me against the world" is their theme song. They trust only themselves and leave everyone else to fend for themselves. I have neighbors, Allen and Mary, who are loners and in their mid-seventies. They say hello if we see them outside, yet they never attend any neighborhood parties or have guests visit. One Saturday morning, we saw an ambulance pull up to the front door. We called over the fence to see what had happened. Mary had passed away unexpectedly. Allen was confused and wanted to talk, so we listened. Mary had health issues, but Allen never realized the severity. Allen spoke to us for over an hour. Then he returned to his home. He accepted some dinners which we passed over the fence but refused any invitations to dine with us. Distrust and solitude continued to consume Allen's world. Human relationships can be painful, yet there is little joy in isolation.

A second path is to immerse oneself in community and

involvement. All your time is devoted to family and friends. You connect and help each other, intertwining in the ever-changing patterns of humanity. Invariably someone will disagree or miscommunicate, and you feel hurt and want to retreat. It is a wild rollercoaster ride of highs and lows. People create human adventure at its finest. We may wish that life was more predictable, hoping that everyone will find the happy middle path one day. Despite the drama, most of us would never choose to become loners.

The third approach is to consider relationships from a higher vantage point. Suppose a higher power created us, gifted us unique talents, and placed us in a specific family and community. I doubt that selection was random. Might there have been a reason, even if we don't understand it? What if both our joys and frustrations are essential? What would it mean to you if this wild speculation were true? What if all people are connected? What could change if we are here to serve each other? Would life be different if our purpose is to help each other?

Mid-life is a perfect vantage point to reflect upon the past and vision the future. Imagine sitting like a child in the middle of a teeter-totter. Only a minor shift in any direction will guide your outcome.

How Did I get Here?

Have you wondered how you ended up with your parents, or considered how your children arrived uniquely different? For years, I thought my parents were an unlikely pair. My mother was a college graduate studying to be a doctor, and my father was a fun-loving high school dropout. My mother was as intense as my father was easy-going. They were an unlikely couple.

My children were distinct individuals, each of them brilliant in their unique ways. You have already learned about my eldest daughter. Corinne was a troubling enigma. My son and younger daughter create their lives, and my job is to encourage them while never knowing the outcome. I have never stopped wondering how I ended up with these people in my life. Parents, siblings, spouses, and children surround me with their energy, drama, and love. We didn't get to choose most of them. Was there a bigger plan?

In his book *Inspiration*, Wayne Dyer relates a conversation he had with God before birth. God asks the yet-to-be-born Wayne what he would like to accomplish on his journey on Earth. Wayne responds, "I'd like to teach self-reliance, compassion, and forgiveness."

God then tells Wayne that the best way to teach him self-reliance is to put him in a series of foster homes where he'll learn to rely upon himself. God separated him from his parents so that he would know inner strength.

Wayne's father was a prisoner, alcoholic, and thief who abandoned him as a baby. Wayne spent many years hating him and wanting revenge. Then, long after his father was gone, Wayne found a way to forgive him, opening the path to teaching forgiveness.

Wayne's mother demonstrated compassion by working for ten years to bring all her children back together.

Wayne was troubled by the suffering of his parents and asks God if their pain is necessary. God tells him that his father had his life request. He signed on to spend his life teaching one of his children forgiveness, while his mother wanted to demonstrate how compassion shows up every day, regardless of circumstances. His parents' lives served a higher purpose. Like pieces to an immense puzzle, Wayne Dyer's inspirational pre-birth vision created meaning for both his pain and his joy. Might we begin to see a pattern as we review the various pieces of life?

What if all that you experience has a plan and a purpose? As you think back on your life, what patterns emerge? How did challenges shape you? When have you felt love? When have you been afraid? Who supported you? What vows did you make to yourself?

Imagine that you were speaking with God before your birth.

- What did you want to experience in this lifetime?
- How did your parents become teachers?
- Where are you on your journey?
- Do you see your purpose emerging?
- What role do your children play?
- What have they taught you?
- What might you have asked from this lifetime?

Wayne Dyer hated his father for more than 30 years of his life. Years after his father's death, he visited his grave. Standing at his father's tombstone, Wayne yelled and flailed, releasing his anger with wild fury. Then in a sudden flash of understanding, Wayne collapsed on the grave with forgiveness. A burst of higher vision provided the inspiration that allowed Wayne to shift into his life of teaching, writing, and speaking to the hearts and souls of millions of people.

It is easy to label relationships as good, bad, supportive, or destructive, yet labels mask the complexity and truth. Ask yourself a more profound question. How could your life have been designed for your benefit? Is this time to change direction? Or to move forward on a clear trajectory?

Your Soul Wish

I have always envied those who had a clear understanding of life's purpose and direction. I'm still working on it. Supporting and nurturing yourself is a lifelong commitment. What do you do if your life purpose is a blur? I know that if you were at sea, you would keep checking the compass and looking for signs. You would notice where the sun comes up and where it sets. You would keep going and do your best to learn something each day. You might also take whatever bits of knowledge you have gathered and leave them like breadcrumbs for others to follow.

My parents provided me with a strange balance of qualities. My mother was a lifelong learner with an interest in medicine and the ability to stretch a dollar. My father was a fun-loving guy who was the life of the party and a student of spiritual and personal development.

As a Little Soul, I suspect that I asked God for a life of continuous learning and the opportunity to teach or share what I found. Spirit chose my parents with wildly different perspectives to challenge me and keep me from over-simplifying. There are many valid ways to look at life. I performed in musical theatre, which taught me how to reinvent myself. With a change of attitude and costume, you can take on a different personality with different outcomes. When I look back, I see my life plan emerge. My life has been and continues to be a thoroughly engaging adventure. It has not been easy. In retrospect, I am fascinated by the twists and turns that looked like a maze of problems to solve.

What might you have requested as a Little Soul? What part of your life provided your challenges? What have you learned along the way? At mid-life, what remains for you? What dreams and visions call you?

Yesterday I was introduced to Joanne, who felt a clear calling since childhood. She wants to make people happy. When she was a child, her parents thought this was wonderful. As she matured into adulthood, they insisted she take life more seriously and prepare for a job. She gave in and took a job. Then in her late forties, Joanne tuned in to her inner voice. In a flash, her heart sang out, and she knew that bringing joy is her gift and calling. Her "soul-ution" was to entertain at conventions until Covid closed them down. With the loss of her income, she searched for new inspiration. Voila! She devised an "adult recess" for companies as an online Zoom offering. She designed a 35-minute work break to give co-workers some simple childlike fun! Businesses loved it. Joanne's recess released stress and created community. Best of all, Joanne is making people happy!

You don't need to push yourself into a narrow box. The first step is listening to your heart. What repeatedly calls to you? What jumps out from social media? What makes you say, "I wish I could do that." Many of us stop this inquiry when we see financial or training obstacles. Yet creativity can blossom when confronted with problems. Find what calls you and put aside the "how" for later.

You may find your passion when you least expect it. I was a mom with three kids when I heard about a local musical theatre group. The vision of singing and dancing on stage captivated me. I took dance classes, but there was a significant obstacle. I had to audition by singing a song. I was terrified. I went to an audition, and my hands shook so badly, I had difficulty signing my name. I was embarrassed by my trembling as I handed my music to the accompanist. When I began to sing, I was almost whispering and swallowed the words. My body froze, standing motionless at center stage. Only when I stopped singing could I move. Time after time, I did not get a callback.

No one else cared whether I was in shows. Yet, I felt driven as I followed my heart. I kept dancing and took singing lessons. I looked for auditions wherever I could find them. For many months I agonized through one miserable audition after another, determined to conquer my fears. Slowly, I improved. I celebrated when I was part of the chorus and continued to learn. Eventually, I acted in minor roles.

What few people understand is that my passion was never about bringing attention to myself. My purpose is to connect the audience with feelings of joy and connection. Music and song join us in spirit. We long for that deeper connection. Words also bring us together, which is why I write.

What has moved you in your life? What draws you forward? When do you feel fully alive? What gifts are you here to share? Now is your time to explore because there is no timetable. If you are already clear on your life purpose, I applaud you and encourage you to become all you can be.

Children Change Us

Motherhood is an extraordinary relationship that goes far beyond birth and caring for a child. It goes beyond upbringing and letting go. I once took a course in self-defense, which demonstrates how motherhood changed me. During this class, we discussed the importance of maintaining an attitude of inner strength. In a threatening situation, looking distracted or weak increases your likelihood of becoming a victim. Our final class exercise was to walk through a park where team members would stalk us for a potential attack. They would attack if they felt our vulnerability.

As I stood at the edge of the park, I envisioned my youngest daughter as a 3-year-old by my side. My love for her expanded into the resolve of a mighty warrior. I felt in my heart that I would die fighting rather than allow anyone to harm her. The attack never came. My energy was palpable. With motherhood comes inner armor. Motherhood is not for the meek.

Then, one day your children grow up. When they announce their independence, they might be 12, 17, or 23, and you recognize that your life will never be the same. While you may always be part of their life, they outgrow the emotional cradle.

Your relationship with your parents may also change as aging parents need your guidance. Alzheimer's and dementia can impact 10% of those over age 65 and 32% of those age 85 and older. Parents with physical impairments may also require assistance. My father suffered from dementia in the last ten years of his life. His humor and wit disappeared as his intellect shriveled. He had the curiosity of a two-year-old. He might take his clothes off outside or poke things into power outlets. One day my mother had tears pouring down her face as she confessed her feelings, "I miss him." I cried with her. My dad was in the room, but his fun-loving smile and warm bear hugs were gone.

Being "sandwiched" between your children and parents may not offer much emotional nourishment. In this time of change, you might explore the unique weave in the fabric of your life. What is perfect about this time? Exploring the bigger picture can provide perspective. How might we see a puzzle where each of us fits together perfectly? What is needed to complete a divine design? What can you offer to others?

In questioning our life and purpose, we could see the people in our lives as obstacles. They distract us, make demands, and pull us in conflicting directions. Yet, none of us find our purpose in a vacuum. How do we deal with the conflicts? I recommend expanding your curiosity. If you are married or in a relationship, you can expect change. Begin by observing your feelings. Ask questions of yourself, as well as the people in your life. What does my husband want? How can we support each other? What is the best path to bring out the best in each of us? Below are several stories of couples working out their future together. Each narrative demonstrates a willingness to step out of a predictable mold and create a life of personal mastery.

Coupling For Life - Two Versions

My friends, Linda and Quincey, decided to give their retirement plans a trial run. Linda had a long and successful career in the travel industry until she lost her job during the pandemic. She hadn't planned on retiring for another five to seven years.

Then 2020 changed her direction. This couple understands the need for a budget, yet they love to travel first class. They researched ways to travel in style and decided to test one possibility. They decided to rent a motor home for four to six months and travel the west. Their adult daughter and husband could move into their parent's house and pay rent. They found a way to travel without the massive expense and return home when they are ready.

They have not yet taken their trip, but this experiment will allow Linda and Quincey to learn whether they like living on the road. Linda can still return to work or retire early. No matter what happens, they will learn about motor home living. Their key to success is creativity and open communication. They enjoy working out their ideas together.

Barbara had a different experience. She had a long marriage to a husband much older. When we met, Barbara was in her early sixties, and her husband was 83 years old. Throughout 25 years of marriage, her husband was continuously building houses. They spent many years living in trailers on the building site during construction. Once the home was complete, they moved in and enjoyed it for a year or so. It was never long before her husband got the "itch" to build, and the cycle would start again. They would sell their home, find a new lot, move into a trailer, and begin building.

Over the years, Barbara's husband became increasingly demanding of her time and attention. When he barked orders, she told him that his behavior was unacceptable, yet he didn't stop. After much prayer and planning, Barbara created a new vision for her life. When her husband acquired a new lot and moved into his trailer, Barbara moved to California, where she could be close to her daughter. Thus began a new lifestyle. With only a limited income from Social Security, she took odd jobs to supplement her income.

Barbara is a master of possibility, always smiling and optimistic. She looks for miracles and finds them. Her job in phone sales travels with her while visiting friends across the nation. Barbara returned to spend time with her husband and took that opportunity to renegotiate their living arrangements. She requested a separate living area, and the couple developed a new respect for each other. After living with her husband for a year, he decided to buy another lot and start building. Barbara, still smiling, took to the road again. Her husband, now in his nineties, continues to build homes.

I admire Barbara's adaptability. She created emotional boundaries and made her needs clear. Her willingness to leave and travel on her own was vital to finding freedom. Both she and her husband felt complete with their solutions. No one lifestyle is suitable for everyone. The best plan for you is one that makes your heart sing.

Retirement Relation Shifts

As you move closer to retirement, most people focus on the financial aspects. Your source of funding is essential, yet planning retirement is much more than a financial plan. Couples need to ask themselves what their life will look like together. If you have both been working, what will happen when you have entire days, weeks, months, and YEARS of living together? Will you need to revamp current habits? Will you change household duties? Do you have passions to share?

Several years ago, I was visiting my aunt and uncle, who were in their nineties. As dinner time approached, my aunt announced that she was leaving to play cards with friends. My uncle would be making dinner for me.

"I cooked for the first 50 years. Now it's his turn to cook for the next 50," my aunt announced as she smiled and went out the door.

My uncle shuffled over to the freezer to pull out a few cardboard boxes. "Would you like an enchilada or lasagna?" he queried while reading the frozen dinner options. I admit that I had anticipated my aunt's meticulous table and fresh entrees. Instead, there were frozen dinners cooked via microwave. Yes, things change.

Taking time to focus on your goals and values is a wake-up call for many. Even when you think you know about your partner, you could be surprised. How long are you willing to work? Do you want to consider retirement in a budget-friendly location? What is crucial to you regarding friends, family, weather, community, hobbies, medical availability, and convenience?

What if you have incompatible plans? How do you feel when you think about spending all day, every day, with your spouse? If you have forgotten how to relate to each other after your "Mom and Dad" roles are over, a therapist may help rekindle the fire. Or you might call it quits.

What If Divorce Is the Path?

For some people, divorce is the path to living the life of your preference. A midlife divorce can free you to discover your heart's desires.

Today, there is little stigma attached to divorce. Currently, 50% of marriages in the US end in divorce. That high rate also means that there are many people over fifty who are available for new relationships. "Senior" online dating is a new option.

As you enter mid-life, you could be questioning past choices. Self-reflection is always valuable. However, thinking "the grass is greener" can be a destructive fantasy on the other side of marriage. I have watched couples work out their issues with mutual respect, allowing them to grow into the best version of themselves. Whenever possible, I recommend this approach.

At times, reconciliation is not possible. In my situation, it was not feasible. When I decided to divorce, I had no visions of bliss in the dating world. I just wanted to escape a soul-deadened world that was without love and respect. I knew that, by myself, life would be better.

Life after divorce is rarely a clean slate, primed for a great relationship. Memories of broken dreams are like crayon scribbles marring the image. Like many newly divorced women, I found it much easier to define what I DIDN'T want.

- I DON'T want to live on a sailboat.
- I DON'T want to be broke.
- I DON'T want to be overweight.

When your focus is on what you want to avoid, it will be hard to move forward. Measuring happiness from the bottom of the barrel is self-defeating. Yet this is a common starting point. I have heard all of the following from women entering the dating world:

- I don't want someone who drives an old car.
- I don't want someone short.
- I don't want someone too tall.
- I don't want a drinker – or a surfer – or an accountant.

You might also hear another version:

- I want someone who drives a new car.
- I want someone over 6' tall.
- I want someone under 6' tall.
- I want a successful business owner.

All the characteristics above are generic and do not define the values or qualities that are essential for your ideal partner. Describing what will make your heart sing requires self-exploration and patience. It may also take time. Be prepared to live alone as you explore and appreciate the unique person you are!

If the thought of divorce has crossed your mind, think carefully. Starting a new life on your terms is not as straightforward or amusing as a sit-com series. It is also not the end of the world. Spending time to learn about yourself is critical. Even a very self-sufficient person may long for a life partner.

In the next chapter, I will share the experience of dating in mid-life. If you are happily married, I celebrate you. If you are questioning your relationship or already on your own, you may find a morality tale. It is all about what we learn in the process.

KEYS FOR REFLECTION:

1. Journal your thoughts about your purpose and your future.
2. Explore ideas for the future with your spouse or with close friends.
3. Take action to clarify your potential direction. Visit places where you may want to retire or take time for activities that may interest you.

Chapter Seven

DATING AT MID-LIFE

"I love you for who I am when we are together. I love us!"
~**Anonymous**

THE DAY I moved out of our home and into my separate apartment, I felt a profound confirmation that I had made the right choice. Floating on my back in the swimming pool, I looked at the moon and felt a deep relief, as though I had taken an elephant off my shoulders. Months later, after I severed my marriage ties, I began to explore the dating world. I was no longer a gawky teen, yet my lack of experience in dating was painful. I married at age twenty and had been a teen when dating. Those times were simple. Dates were usually a dance or a movie. The boys asked, the girls accepted.

At age 48, I had no idea what to expect. Dating was not simple, and I was no longer a clueless youngster. Adults arrive for a date with truckloads of life experience and expectations. Dates never come alone. They bring a long trail of connections:

children, grandchildren, former spouses, health concerns, geographic and political preferences, and money habits.

I was ready to embark on this new challenge. I couldn't resist evaluating whether my date was good-looking, and surprisingly, I found that streaks of silver hair qualified as "cute." More surprises lay in store for me. I thought I was looking for love but found self-discovery, clarity, and learned to love the better parts of myself. I had opportunities to meet people who helped me become more compassionate, loving, and accepting of the unique gift that each person offers.

For me, dating was a journey to a foreign land. After years of weekends at soccer games or evenings when I was performing in musical theatre, I found myself speechless when a new date asked, "What do you like to do for fun?" My earlier activities weren't date friendly. In the following years I learned that I like concerts in the park, dinners at a local café, wine tasting, movies, educational lectures, vacations on warm beaches, and good times with friends. I began to smile more and expand my world.

I permitted myself to explore what is important to me. I could decorate my apartment without consulting anyone. I hung beach hats on a wall near my bed without concern that anyone would find them too "girly." I learned to appreciate my moods, develop a personal code of conduct, and be honest with my feelings. I spent fifteen years as a single, and apparently, I needed that time of learning.

After decades of married life, returning to the dating world is like going to a ski slope for the first time. I didn't know what to do, what equipment I needed, whether it fit properly, and who to ask for guidance. I showed up and did the best I could.

My first dating strategy was to seek the opposite of what I disliked. Since I felt that my ex-husband was irresponsible with money, I did not want to repeat THAT mistake. I wasn't looking for a knight in shining armor. My approach was like placing a bullseye target on the wall and declaring myself a winner if I DIDN'T hit the mark!

Naturally, it was not difficult to find dates that fit my vague description. They could have been controlling, stingy, irritable, or dull - I wouldn't have noticed. If Prince Charming could balance his checking account, he fit my dating criteria. Consequently, my dating pool was wide open.

Along came fiscally responsible Kevin. He drove a broken-down car with a driver's side door that wouldn't open. Out of necessity, I went around and opened HIS door. In a pinch, he lent me some money. Naturally, he had me sign a note and make payments. I didn't blame him. He was fiscally responsible. Incidentally, I had no mention of romance on my "perfect date" checklist. Keep in mind that I hadn't dated in 25 years, so I was out of practice. When Kevin and I broke up, I thought romance might be a desirable request to add to my list. That opened the door for Alan and Ted.

Silver-Haired Fox Hunters

Next came the dream who walked right out of a romantic novel. Alan had wavy hair, a firm body, and peppered our conversation with scintillating references to sex. He shared his psychological drama once he learned that I am a coach trained in mindset and excellence. I was speechless to learn that his mother had seduced him when Alan was a young teen, and he continued to carry the burden. However, he also continued to visit his mom for *very intimate* mother/son time together. Gulp! That was the end of the story for me. Alan eventually found a woman who looked like his mother, and his story ended happily for all three consenting adults. I was happy NOT to be part of the drama.

Then came Ted. Online dating had educated my tastes, and I had a new deal-breaker. I would only date men who knew how to SPELL. Ted could not only spell, but he was also a talented comedy-writer. As a former English major, I admired his versatility with words. He sent me clever messages, which made me laugh. Ted was witty and entertaining, and I was enthralled.

Ted was a romantic. He took me for picnics on the beach and dropped in unexpectedly because he missed me. Ted sent me cute notes asking me to come over. I was so enthralled with Ted's clever banter that it was several months before I noticed that he never scheduled time in advance. Instead, he would "drop in" for a romantic interlude. It occurred to me that we never spent time in public. What was going on?

I began to wonder how I allowed this to happen. I sought out a therapist to help me with my dating strategy. I wanted to understand why I was tolerating a lack of consideration. Then I had a dream which I shared with my therapist. I envisioned myself as a doormat, with Ted wiping his feet on me.

The subconscious message was clear. I had become a welcome mat for Ted. With support from my therapist, I learned to set boundaries and make requests. Ted stopped his visits and disappeared.

The world of online dating is a strange fantasyland. Ted reappeared six years later. I had a new picture, and to my surprise, he sent me the SAME clever note to connect. With forced humility, I recognized that Ted had utterly forgotten me. We spoke on the phone, and it was the same old Ted. I told him I was open to date IF he called ahead. That never happened. Time adds perspective to experience, and I learned genuine gratitude. Because of Ted, I hired a therapist to move my life forward. Wisdom and personal progress often come from unintended sources.

Several years ago, a recently single friend commented on a clever note she received from a dating site. This gentleman had a boat and loved picnics on the beach. He was highly creative and funny. I blurted out, "Is his name Ted?"

You guessed it. After reading Ted's email, we recognized that he is still single and dangling the same bait. It was the SAME email he had sent me twice. Ted's marketing campaign hit the target! He could change the name of the girl and keep the punchlines. It is a proven technique, so why change? This time the joke was on him. I shared his M.O. with my friend, and the game was off.

I learned that sharing dating experiences with girlfriends is a wise idea. You can save each other some unnecessary learning experiences. My friend Patty told me about a man who owned a beautiful home in Hawaii but frequently visited Southern California. Mr. Aloha sounded perfect. He invited my friend to a nice restaurant. After dinner, Patty excused herself to go to the bathroom. As she returned, he was waiting in the restaurant phone alcove. He pulled her next to him and became very sexually aggressive. As she resisted, she noticed that the servers were intentionally not noticing. She broke away and never spoke with him again. When Mr. Aloha showed up in my dating inbox, he looked interesting. Then he invited me to meet him at the very same restaurant where he assaulted my friend. I passed.

Another silver fox with a supply of Viagra enticed my friend, Eve. She lost her husband to cancer several years earlier and was ready to date again. When I asked what she was looking for, she had only one criterion: tall.

Eve was visiting a friend with a home near the beach in Mexico. As she walked the beach, a man on a white horse galloped up through the surf. The sun flashed across his silver hair, and he rode close to Eve. When he dismounted and flexed his muscles, Eve thought she was in a movie. She was in love.

Greg introduced himself and invited her to dinner and later to bed that night. Eve was ecstatic. She came home, thrilled with her encounter. Within 24 hours, Eve began to wonder why he wasn't calling her every night. By Wednesday, she was becoming desperate. Then he called and scheduled a visit for the following weekend.

Eve got another charge of oxytocin and romantic ecstasy. The following week, Greg didn't call. Eve called him several times to leave messages, but he didn't initiate contact. Although Eve is a beautiful woman, she doubted herself as she imagined why he hadn't called. First, Eve listed everything that might be wrong with her. She was resolute in the belief that she had to change to find Mr. Wonderful. She then recognized that Greg was not a "forever" type guy, so Eve convinced herself to enjoy sex without attachment. Eve spent another night with Greg and came home very proud of her "liberation." Her experiment lasted for less than 24 hours before she collapsed in tears, waiting for a phone call.

It took several months of painful self-talk before Eve realized that Greg dedicated himself to sweeping women off their feet. He liked sex but had no desire for a relationship. Eve recognized that she needed more than a tall man. She wanted a commitment and phone calls.

Dating Lesson Number One

Your focus determines your outcome. When expectations are low, your chances of finding a date are high. I wanted someone the opposite of my ex-husband. Eve wanted someone tall. If that were all we needed, we might have been happy. We learned that our hearts and minds long for much more. Dating failures help us discover what we need in a supportive and lasting partnership. Dating is an opportunity to learn more about yourself.

Author and speaker, Michael Beckwith, says it best: "No one ever breaks our heart. They break our expectations." When a relationship doesn't work out, we uncover our hidden expectations. It is only then that we can be honest about what we want and need. If you are dating, learn to be patient and forgiving. You may have multiple learning experiences which bring clarity on what is vitally important.

After my first dating flops, I added more criteria. I made a list of characteristics for my ideal partner:

- Fiscally responsible
- Sense of humor
- Healthy/takes care of himself
- Likes the beach
- Considerate

- Entrepreneurial
- Non-smoker

With this list, I had more learning experiences:

- One date met me at Starbucks for an initial meeting. He brought a newspaper with an extensive real-estate section. He greeted me with a kiss like a long-lost lover and began to look for our home in the local newspaper. That was our first and last date. Too much, too fast. I didn't know anything about him.
- A psychologist wanted to get to know me by asking about the "worst things that ever happened to me." That day I learned that history might be defined by the events of the past. However, character is defined by an individual's mental and moral response. Painful experiences can drop us into despair or strengthen our will, expanding our compassion and resolve. You and I are much more than our history.
- I dated a smoker who hid his habit from me because he knew that I preferred a non-smoker. After a month, he shared that he smoked, but only outdoors. I considered the possibility that his smoking wasn't a deal-breaker after all. By our second month of dating, he resented smoking outside. And I became concerned about his health because I started to like him. One night he flew into a rage because he didn't want to smoke outside, and I recognized that I couldn't live with a smoker. It was over.
- I spent time with several male friends who kept me

sane. Lou took walks with me and talked about spiritual growth. He constantly challenged me to learn more. Adam went to personal development events with me. Even though he had girlfriends, he was playful, and we had fun at the beach or sharing pizza, like two young kids. Gene was a coach who was always enthusiastic. He was chronically late for everything, but we went to the movies and talked about our challenges. I highly recommend having non-romantic male energy in your life. Perhaps you have a brother or friends you have known for years. It is a relief to spend time with good men without any romantic complications.

After being single for more than a decade, I gradually developed clarity, allowing honest and authentic conversations with dates. I shared my life vision from my heart. And I knew that the right man for me would have the lovable qualities of my three male friends, but without their issues. Lou had poor health. Adam had sporadic uncontrollable anger, and Gene's procrastination and chronic tardiness would all be fatal problems in a relationship. My time was coming.

Finding the ONE to Love

The most important relationship you will ever have is with yourself. Mid-life relationship changes bring you to center stage. Nothing else will work until YOU become the person you love and respect. Half your life is past and what remains is precious. Looking in the rear-view mirror, I recognized how I shapeshifted to fit the expectations of others. I played multiple roles: daughter, wife, and mother. I put my vision and values dead last.

Dating allowed me to learn what I needed to feel whole. I peeled off my artificial mask and exposed my authentic strength and character. Dating taught me how to respect myself and others. I learned that dating did not need to be complicated or painful. I met fellow human beings who were also seeking their one special person to love. We could be honest with each other without disrespect or blame when the chemistry wasn't there.

The final key to my happiness came unexpectedly. I dated Carl for several months. I thought we were getting along until he began to disengage. I felt hurt and asked what was wrong. He told me that I was too optimistic. We broke up. I had never thought that optimism was a fault.

The next man I dated lasted about six months. When we called it quits, he gave me the same critique: I AM TOO OPTI-MISTIC! These words stopped me in my tracks. Two different men had the same issue with me.

I admit to having character flaws. I have unfiled papers in my office, I leave dust on the furniture, and forget to return phone calls. But optimism is key to waking happy every morning and looking forward to a terrific day! Optimism is a quality that I LOVE in myself. Stop right here! I discovered and declared a personal characteristic that I LOVE! This unequivocal approval felt like a badge of honor. At long last, I felt free from the opinion of others. I may not be perfect, but I don't need to change to please anyone else. I felt a deep connection with the spirit that created me.

I sat in nature and had a conversation with God. I thanked

God for putting those two men in my life to expose the depth of my heart. I fell in love with myself. I felt complete, knowing that I would rather live by myself with my optimism than escape into a second-rate relationship. Here is what I said to God.

Dear God:

I am grateful for my ability to wake up happy and optimistic. I thank you for showing me that peace of mind. You know that in my heart, I want a life partner. You also understand what truly serves me. I want a partner that uplifts me.

I put my future in your hands. Beginning now, I am eliminating all computer dating. Instead, I choose to create a community around me and support others to express the best of themselves. I surrender to your will.

If a partner contributes to my life purpose, then please put him in front of me. He will find me, wherever I am, even as I live life to the fullest.

With love and gratitude for the life you have given me,

Carole

Something inside of me had changed. True to my word, I stopped internet dating and any search for a mate. I made plans to move to the San Diego area because it made me happy. I met a single girlfriend named Ronnie at a seminar, and we discussed sharing an apartment near the beach. We decided to discuss it further at another conference several weeks later.

When I found her at the conference, Ronnie told me that she

couldn't have dinner to discuss the apartment. That is when God stepped in. Ronnie and I both knew a single man named Paul. He overheard our discussion and asked me to join him for dinner. That dinner was the beginning of our profoundly loving and supportive relationship, which led to marriage.

God takes care of the details when you trust. Paul did not appear when I wanted. He came when I was ready. Paul brought the qualities and values that my heart craved: deep emotional support, common worldview, focus on healthful eating and living, a quirky sense of humor and childlike antics (like my own), and the depth to commit for a lifetime. I had reached maturity and confidence within myself to accept Paul's physical limitations and challenges. Ten years earlier, I could not have moved past these issues.

The keys to happiness in both your love life and your financial life are similar:

- Take time to know what you want.
- Learn from your experience.
- Appreciate the good in your life. A price tag doesn't determine value. You measure value by the fullness in your heart.
- Create your life vision, and within it, you will find your purpose.
- Learn to love yourself with the care you would give to a sensitive child in your care – with kindness and thoughtful action.

Once you have developed this clarity, you give your dreams the roadmap and the financial legs to run like the wind.

Paul and I have now been married for seven years. We have a vibrant and fully expressive relationship. We got married in a small ceremony with our families in attendance. It was perfect for us. I include our vows here both for their sense of fun and the more profound expression of who we are:

PAUL'S PROMISE TO "MY BELOVED, CAROLE."

- I promise to love, honor, and cherish you even in times of misunderstandings and disagreements.
- I promise to be faithful and loving all the days I have left on earth.
- I promise to be crazy, playful, and smile a lot when you are with me.
- I promise to listen as best as I can when you need a sounding board without interrupting you. It would be helpful to call my name and get my attention first since my hearing aid doesn't work very well.
- I promise to rub your feet and legs whenever you drop them in my lap.
- I promise to work hard and create the lifestyle you deserve.
- I promise to take care of myself and become strong, virile, and healthy.

Carole's promise to Paul

- I promise to love you and hold you as the loving and committed person I know you to be.
- I promise to be authentic and open in our communication so that our relationship will continue to grow.
- I promise to listen when you need to be heard.
- I promise to step aside when you want to yell at the computer and the inadequacies of Microsoft.
- I promise to understand and give you solitude when you need to be alone. And to know I can always go shopping instead.
- I promise to allow you space to be fully self-expressed while encouraging you to keep your collection of stuffed animals and blue crystal out of the living room and in your area.
- I promise to hold you and touch you when you want to be held and touched.
- I promise to understand and make room for your humanness, with both its strengths and weaknesses.
- I promise to be understanding when you put ketchup on pasta.
- I promise to be patient when you compare prices for anything over $1.
- I promise to remember that you don't like any restaurants except Subway and Soup Plantation, so I shouldn't be surprised when you complain about going anywhere else. I will also remember that you

are supportive and encourage me to go out to restaurants with my sisters and girlfriends instead.

- I promise to be appreciative when you fix anything that breaks.
- I promise to be thrilled that you are a loving partner who does the dishes voluntarily, even when I have used all the pots and pans.
- I love having someone a little crazy who (like me) ENJOYS going to seminars and timeshare presentations.
- I am forever grateful that God brought us together, and we see our unity, even when we are sometimes an odd couple. Paul, I love you for just who you are. I trust that together we create a life adventure worth sharing, with lots of fun and laughter along the way.

KEYS FOR REFLECTION:
Taking charge of your relationship

1. What qualities are most important to you in a relationship?
2. What qualities do you love about yourself?
3. How can you be a better parent to yourself?
4. What will make your future most fulfilling?
5. How can you and your partner have an authentic conversation about your future together?
6. Make a list of your retirement goals and ask your partner to do the same. Choose a relaxed time to review your lists together. Do this with love.

Part Two

MIND YOUR MONEY

"Money is only a tool. It will take you wherever you wish, but it will not replace you as the driver."
~Ayn Rand

Chapter Eight

THE SPIRIT OF MONEY

"You are not a drop in the ocean. You are the ocean in a single drop."

~Rumi

MONEY IS NOT what it seems to be. Even after you learn the basics and build a personal net worth, you may find that money is elusive. Hard work does not guarantee money, and neither is money denied to those who seem to ignore it.

While we still visualize money as a stack of green bills, money is now a number stored in the cloud. You may have dollars, yen, Amazon credits, or Bitcoin. Money can be elusive yet necessary for daily life. To learn more about the history of money, see APPENDIX 1.

What does Money Mean to You?

Let's turn to self-evaluation. What does money mean to you? How does it impact your family, community, work, and society? Do you find anything unique in your view of money?

I once thought of money as "mine" as opposed to "yours." In a family, it grew to be "our money." I acknowledge how money flows in and out of my life. I admit that I spend my time blocking the "outflow" of money as I look for every opportunity for a sale or deal. How about you? What might happen if we directed more focus to increase income and inflow? What do you observe about the way that money moves through your life?

Let's go deeper. What is the purpose of money in human life? Could it be a device to bring us together? The earth is a BIG place. What would promote cooperation, brainstorming, and diverse perspective? Beginning with barter, people learned that life was better when you traded goods and services, sharing your skills. Money allows us to prosper while contributing goods and services to each other. In a spiritual sense, this exchange helps bind us together.

I encourage you to expand your views about money. If you are a mother, you have observed that each of your children is special and unique. The children of the world also bring their unique gifts. How might we harness this genius for the well-being of all?

What becomes possible if all citizens have the basics, like food and shelter? Some people feel that everyone would become lazy if they didn't live in fear and dissatisfaction. Is that true? Is healthcare a basic necessity? Or only for those with high incomes? Have recent events shifted your view? Can we make meaningful changes in healthcare delivery? What is working well? And for whom? Who is left out? What is our responsibility?

How do we compare with other countries? Is there something we can learn? Do other countries have systems we can emulate? What is our standard of excellence? Is money the critical factor? Are other forces at play? What part does culture play? What other questions should we be asking?

The Spirit of Money is always at work. The spirit within you responds as you develop curiosity and question the status quo. The questioning mind and heart can find answers to make the world a better place.

"If we have no peace, it is because we have forgotten that we belong to each other."

~Mother Teresa

KEYS FOR REFLECTION:
There are many ideas in this chapter. Take a few moments to digest their meaning for yourself.

1. What ideas in this chapter appealed to you?
2. Did any ideas upset you? Did deeper into your background to discover the source of the upset.
3. How does this impact your view of money?

Chapter Nine

IS SOCIAL SECURITY YOUR SECURITY?

"Cherish the friends, moments, and treasures that make you smile. Invest them where they will support you all the days of your life!"
~Carole Hodges

MOST PEOPLE HAVE an unacknowledged program for their life. It shows up when planning for retirement. When I speak with someone about finances, we begin with two figures: 1. your "run rate" or your estimated annual expense; 2. the number of years you will live. Multiply these two figures to arrive at the amount of income you require for the remainder of your life. I find that everyone has an estimate for their "expiration date."

Of course, we don't know when we will die. But by mid-life, people have a hunch how long they will live. When I ask someone how long their retirement savings must last, they pause for a moment and then offer an answer. A majority of people expect to live until their eighties or nineties. A few anticipate living beyond 100. Most consider their current state of health and the age that their parents or relatives have passed. This personal belief underlies their financial plans and can become a self-fulfilling prophecy.

Your personal life projection changes as you age. In my twenties, I couldn't imagine myself at 35 or 40. By the time I was 50, I had developed a vision of myself into old age. My number is 104, which is a feeling more than a logical calculation. I plan for an active life right up to my earthly departure.

When you ask your intuition how long you will live, what is the response? What must you do in your remaining years to live fulfilled? Do you sense that anything will change in the last ten years of your life? Are you busy, active, and involved now? Or are you relaxed and reflective while enjoying the beauty of the earth and your family? After you retire, where might you be living and with whom?

Keep these ideas in mind as you consider the practical details of retirement. There are no awards for the best retirement plan. You decide when it is right for you. If you were to die at 68, you might want to live extravagantly or leave a legacy. If you were to die at 98, you might want to ensure that you have a good cash flow right to the end. And, of course, you will want to have funds for medical expenses, which can pop up unexpectedly at any age! As you learn more, review your expectations about social security, pensions, and retirement savings like 401K, IRA, and Roth IRA.

The Basics of Social Security

One day when you open the mail, you will find a notice from

the US Government announcing that you are eligible for Social Security. If you have worked in the United States for a <u>minimum</u> of ten years and contributed to FICA each paycheck, you are entitled to Social Security. FICA stands for the Federal Insurance Contributions Act. You and your employer both pay FICA taxes which include Social Security and Medicare contributions. Your employer matches your contribution. Your tax contributions over many years entitle you to receive a monthly Social Security payment for the remainder of your life.

President Franklin D. Roosevelt signed the Social Security Act on August 14, 1935. In the 1930s, the population shifted from rural areas into cities to find jobs. During the Great Depression, many people were laid off and withdrew their retirement savings to survive. These premature withdrawals left many people without resources as they became elderly. Social Security provided a safety net for the elderly as well as disability and unemployment benefits.

Although Roosevelt signed Social Security into law more than 85 years ago, it is still a safety net for the elderly. While it is called an "entitlement" program, only those who have paid into the program for a minimum of ten years are eligible. Your monthly Social Security payments are based upon the average income of your highest 35 years. To qualify for this retirement benefit, you be a citizen OR show proof of your right to live in the USA with evidence of your earnings and FICA contributions. There is no free ride for Social Security except for the non-working spouse and disabled or underage children.

Now let's get to the critical part. What will Social Security mean for your retirement? You can check on your current earnings by going to SSA.gov and selecting "My Social Security" account. The first time you log in, you'll need to access your account by providing a username and password. This account will give you a record of your lifetime earnings. It may also give you an estimate of your Social Security benefit based on your current earnings. SS payments will change as you continue to work and contribute to your social security account. The amount of your monthly social security is also determined by the age you start receiving your monthly benefit.

Here is the maximum monthly payment in 2022.

Claim at age 62	$2,364
Claim at full retirement	$3,568 (age 67 if born after 1960)
Claim at age 70	$4194

These estimates apply to workers who have contributed the maximum to Social Security. However, the **average** Social Security benefit in 2022 is $1657 per month. Each year, Social Security evaluates the cost of living and makes adjustments. Your starting base impacts all future increases. A 2% increase per year over 20 years looks like this:

Initial Benefit	After an increase of 2% over 30 years
$1,657	$2,943
$2,364	$4,168
$3,568	$6,336
$4,194	$7,448

As you can see, if you wait until age 70 before claiming your Social Security, you will receive the highest benefit. However, that doesn't mean it is the right decision for you. You can do the math for yourself. To calculate your lifetime Social Security income, multiply your annual distribution by the number of years you expect to collect SSI.

Some people have health or genetic issues that impact their longevity. If you don't expect to live into your seventies, you may wish to retire early. Conversely, if you anticipate living into your eighties or even over 100, you might choose to work longer or delay your benefit. Social security is a lifetime benefit that you cannot outlive. Your supplemental retirement savings may not have these guarantees.

Evaluate your Social Security distribution carefully. Calculate your options by estimating how long you expect to live. Then make a personal choice that supports your health, finances, and peace of mind. Get specific details at My Social Security.com and review your records. Keep in mind that you will also increase your SSI benefit when you increase your income between now and your retirement age.

Check Social Security benefits, go to https://ssa.gov. Review your income record and see where you stand now.

Pensions and 401K

Before 1980, many companies provided defined benefit pension plans that provided employees who worked for 20-30 years with a guaranteed pension. The employer took responsibility for funding this benefit as a reward for lifetime service.

The retirement landscape began to shift with the advent of the 401k in 1978. Workers could choose to set aside tax-deferred income for retirement. It was appealing to lower current income taxes as an incentive to save for the future. Over time the 401k replaced pensions. Companies that were financially burdened by pension guarantees preferred to contribute to a 401k plan. It was better for the bottom line. Employees liked the ability to keep their retirement savings when they changed employers. And technology gave both employers and employees access to investment choices for their 401K savings.

Pensions began to disappear. Today's pensions are primarily for teachers, government workers, police, firefighters, and the military. If you have a retirement pension, start early to research your benefit. Pension benefits may include spousal support in the event of death or disability. Military pensions may begin after twenty years of service regardless of your age. Contact your company, union, or pension administrator to learn the details. Verify your pension guarantees.

What happens if you have eligibility for a pension and worked for ten years or more at a company where you paid FICA taxes or paid into a 401K? You could collect both a pension and Social Security as well as having your retirement savings! Be aware that Social Security has a "Windfall Elimination Provision," which prevents "double-dipping." You will need to confirm your status through Social Security.

Knowing the details of your 401K, pension, and Social Security can make a significant difference. I worked with a teacher who decided to work a few extra years until age 70 because it triggered substantial extra Social Security income for her. Your circumstances may be quite different from others. Gather your specific information and review your situation with Social Security and your financial advisors.

Today, most employees have access to a 401K plan. Employers set up their company plan. All employee contributions are voluntary, based upon choosing a percentage of income for automatic transfer into their 401K account. Many companies offer to match a portion of the employee's contribution.

An example of a company match is 6% of income for the employee's 401K plan. An employee contributing 3% of her income would receive an additional 3% in matching funds; an employee contributing 8% of pay to her 401K would get the 6% maximum company match. Your company match is free money for you. It is wise to set your contribution to equal or exceed the company's match.

All 401K employee contributions are tax-deductible in the year that you make them. In other words, you do not pay tax on this income UNTIL you withdraw it. Your employer's contribution is also free from income tax. Taxes ARE required on your withdrawals and play a substantial role in retirement income strategy. If you can optimize your tax-free funds, you can increase your spendable income in retirement. In future chapters, we will review several tax-free options.

WARNING: Many Americans have minimal savings, and their 401K plan is their largest savings reservoir. Taking money from your 401K becomes a temptation when a financial need arises. Withdrawing 401K reserves can be a costly trap that robs you of your retirement savings. There is a 10% penalty for withdrawing your 401K savings before age 59 ½, AND YOU MUST PAY THE INCOME TAX on your withdrawals. When you are desperate for money, taxes may not seem like a problem. Only later will you recognize that you have lost money and a piece of your future.

For example, if you are single, earning $50,000, and withdraw $20,000 from your 401K, you would receive only $15,600 after paying $4,400 in penalties and taxes.

If you must tap into your 401K for an emergency, there is a better alternative. You can borrow your 401K funds. While you will pay interest, you will not be subject to penalties and taxes, which makes a significant difference in the value of your savings. And you do not lose interest, because you pay yourself! Your payments go back into your 401K savings. There are some restrictions on 401K loans. You must be an active employee and repay the loan within five years. When you safeguard your future, you receive emotional dividends as well.

Each employer establishes their 401K and the range of investments. You have limited choices. Be aware that you have fees for maintaining your 401K deducted from your account. Take time to study your plan to make the most of this invest-ment. Some companies allow you to transfer some or all your 401K savings to a different manager. By learning your options, you can make intelligent choices.

Roth IRA & 401K

Your 401K contributions save you taxes now and grow tax deferred. The Roth IRA and 401K allow you to accumulate tax-free savings and make tax-free withdrawals later. "What is the catch?" you may ask.

- You pay taxes on income that you contribute to your Roth account.
- Roth IRA has limits on your annual contributions.

Yet, the Roth IRA provides tax-free income later in life. If you were a farmer, this would be like paying tax on the seed rather than the crop.

You may not participate in a Roth 401K unless your employer offers that choice. Many large employers offer both the traditional and the Roth. The amount of money you can contribute is the same – often $18,500 - $24,000 annually. I recently read that six out of ten employees are choosing the Roth 401K. By paying tax on this contribution now, you will have more money to spend during retirement.

You may also set up an Individual Roth IRA for your after-tax contributions at a wide assortment of many financial institutions. There are annual limits for Roth IRA contributions. For the tax year ending 2020, the limits are:

- $6,000 if you're younger than age 50
- $7,000 if you're aged 50 or older

You may only contribute earned income from a job or self-employment to a Roth IRA. Money from rental property, unemployment, Social Security, or pensions will not qualify as earned income. You pay tax on this income before making your contribution. Your contributions must be held in your Roth IRA for a minimum of five years before a tax-free withdrawal. Unlike the 401K, there are no "Required Minimum Distributions" (RMD), so you are in control of your distributions. Withdrawal flexibility is a real benefit for good money management.

You are wise to think ahead regarding your retirement income. Before making any decision that impacts your financial future, you can benefit from speaking with professionals to explore facts and understand your options. There are no guarantees that your 401K, Roth 401K, or Roth IRA will give positive returns. Your investment choices may lose money in a down market. Choose wisely!

Your Home in Retirement

If you own your own home, you have a significant asset. How will this help you in retirement? As you reduce your mortgage and the value of your property increases, your investment grows. How might you use this asset to support your retirement? Here are a few ideas.

1. A home equity line of credit or refinanced mortgage can provide additional funds. When interest rates are low, this might be appealing. However, you will increase your monthly expenses.
2. You might sell your home and downsize or move to another area.
3. You could take out a reverse mortgage on your home.

Many people set a goal to pay off their mortgage before they retire. Eliminating a mortgage payment makes sense in retirement. Even if you have a mortgage, it is a fixed amount. A renter must be concerned about rent increases. Homeownership can provide a feeling of security.

Now consider the expenses of homeownership.

- Home maintenance and repairs. When the water heater leaks or someone breaks a window, you pay.
- Home and liability insurance.
- Property Taxes. As the value of your home goes up, you will also get a larger tax bill.

Some people mistakenly think that they can ignore some prudent overhead expenses. One owner decided to eliminate home insurance after paying off his mortgage because the lender no longer required insurance. This widower lived in a remote rural area surrounded by brush. Both the fire risk and the cost of fire insurance were high. Enraged at the expense of fire insurance, the owner canceled his home insurance. That could prove to be a costly decision. His home is his primary asset, and without fire insurance, he wouldn't have funds to rebuild. Ill-informed people think they can purchase insurance once an active fire is moving toward their home. The reality is that no insurance company will cover them when a threat is imminent.

Another individual stopped paying property taxes on his home after eliminating the mortgage. As property tax bills arrived, he ignored them. After years of notices, the County auctioned the property to pay the past-due taxes. A new buyer purchased the home and posted a three-day eviction notice on the front door. All possessions had to be out within three days, or the locks would be changed, and anything remaining became the new owner's property.

The original owner had to find an apartment and move in a hurry. Years later, he received partial compensation. The county sold his house at auction for significantly more than the overdue property tax. After deducting taxes, interest penalties, legal, and processing fees, the former owner received the balance. The loss of home equity and the stress of a sudden move was immense. The lesson is to treat property taxes as essential bills. Often there are better options. He might have borrowed the funds with a small mortgage or sold the home at a competitive price and voluntarily downsized.

Your home may be your largest single asset and critical to your financial future. Your home might fund part of your retirement as well as providing you comfort.

If you plan to live in your home indefinitely, you might consider updating or remodeling to increase its value and your enjoyment. A home equity line or a new mortgage can make the expense affordable. Do your research on both the cost of upgrades and the potential increase in value. Keep in mind that home projects often include an element of surprise, such as rebuilding a foundation or replacing electrical or plumbing systems.

One popular way to access your equity is to sell your home and move to a smaller home or a less expensive state. You may pay taxes on some of the profit. Check the capital gains laws on the sale of your home. Currently, $250,000 of gain is tax-free if you have lived in the house for two of the five years before the sale. If you are married and file a joint return, the tax-free amount doubles to $500,000.

Moving to a less expensive area can be a happy choice when you are ready to retire. Check lifestyle details in advance. I live in California, where home prices are high. Friends have moved to Arizona or Michigan and been delighted when they found a home they could purchase for a fraction of California prices. However, they neglected to consider the expense of cooling or heating. The cost of living can change significantly by location. The weather, cost of transportation, (will you need a new car with snow tires?), as well as the cost of food, travel, entertainment, and utilities, will impact your monthly expense. Learn about homeownership laws in your new location. The rules vary, and you will want to avoid future surprises.

If you love your home and want to live there for the rest of your life, you might consider a reverse mortgage. I have heard misconceptions about reverse mortgages. Some people are afraid that the bank will repossess their homes and force them out in their old age. The reality is that a reverse mortgage can be a guarantee to keep you in your home for your lifetime. To be eligible for a reverse mortgage, one owner must be at least 62 years of age. You also must have 35% or more equity in your property and intend to live at the property. Rental properties are not eligible for a reverse mortgage.

A reverse mortgage could

- eliminate your mortgage payments
- give you cash that you don't need to pay back
- pay you monthly

A reverse mortgage is an option for those who need to access money from their home without a repayment plan. It can bring comfort to homeowners who do not have sufficient retirement income to live securely. A reverse mortgage allows the owner to access the equity in their home while living in it.

Even if a reverse mortgage eliminates any mortgage payment, the homeowner must pay property taxes and home maintenance. And the owner may sell the house in the future and receive any remaining equity. If the owner dies with remaining home equity, a will or trust can name beneficiaries. Essentially, the reverse mortgage is an increasing loan each month based on interest rates and the owner's payments. Not all homes are eligible for a reverse mortgage. Researching your specific situation can give you peace of mind.

Once you identify your options, you can feel more confident about your retirement. Speak with professionals: a realtor, mortgage broker, investment advisor, estate planner, and insurance specialist can bring you a well-rounded perspective. Most professionals want the best for their clients and will disclose any potential bias due to personal interest. Ask questions and plan carefully. Invite your children to participate as well.

KEYS FOR REFLECTION:
MAKE A RETIREMENT CHECKLIST

1. Plan Social Security – check annually starting by age 50.
2. Understand pensions if you have access to any.
3. Grow and protect your 401K.
4. Consider Roth IRA and Roth 401k benefits – non-taxable – no RMD.
5. Real Estate benefits and liabilities:

  - Equity is an asset
  - Ways to use your equity – sale – refinance
  - Reverse mortgage
  - Upkeep expenses
  - Property taxes

Chapter Ten

CREATING MONEY FOR LIFE

"Life is what happens when you're busy making other plans."
~John Lennon

LET'S come back to evaluate your present net worth. What if your wealth determined your longevity? Quite simply, how long could you live on the money you now have if you stopped getting additional money today?

For most people, the answer is "much less than one year." For many, it is less than a month or a week. Americans are not great savers, and sudden unemployment highlights the need for emergency savings. Last year, when incomes stopped, food lines grew to previously unimagined lengths.

Revisiting Net-Worth

Consider that not all your wealth is liquid or readily available. A universal measure of wealth is net worth, which includes stored wealth such as:

- equity in your home or other real property
- future inheritance
- stocks and bonds
- retirement plans like 401k or pension
- permanent life insurance policies
- annuities
- business value
- automobiles
- art collections
- jewelry
- collections

These assets have a monetary value to be included in your net worth. The formula is simple:

ASSETS minus LIABILITIES = NET WORTH

Let's review the process to calculate your financial net worth:

1. List the current value of everything you own:

- Money in your bank accounts
- Value of your investment accounts
- Cars
- The market value of your home and other properties
- Business value
- Personal property such as jewelry, art, furniture, collections

- Cash value of permanent life insurance

2. List your liabilities (everything you owe):

- Mortgage(s)
- Car loan(s)
- Credit card balances
- Student loans

3. Subtract what you owe from the value of your assets

THE RESULT IS YOUR NET WORTH

This number frequently changes. List assets based upon their current market value. Your car is likely to have a lower value than when you bought it. Your home may have a higher value than its purchase price. These calculations will shift up and down. Your net worth is an indicator of where you spend money and store financial reserve. It reflects your current choices.

When you retire and relinquish employment income, you will rely on Social Security, pensions, 401K, IRA, investments, and savings to cover living costs. To balance your retirement, you can lower your expenses or increase your income. We have already discussed ways to reduce housing expenses by moving or by getting a reverse mortgage. Now let's look at some other alternatives:

- Investment income
- Finding non-taxable income

- Guaranteed income for the remainder of your life
- Rental income
- Using your skills

If you are more than a decade away from retirement, you still have time to create a workable plan. The time to act is now. Some of these choices have an expiration date.

Your skills are also assets. You may have specialized knowledge such as understanding people or technology, valuable experience to share, artistic or writing talent. How might you create additional income?

- The Bureau of Labor Statistics estimated that 26% of people between 64 and 74 were working in 2016, and likely to increase to 30% by 2026.
- They also found that 8.4% of people 75 or older were working, anticipating an increase to 10.8% by 2026.

Is working part of your retirement plan? Or is it your backup plan? Consider your choices carefully. Time is only on your side if you begin when you are young and you will never be younger than today. Every decade you wait reduces your options. Are there skills you want to learn today to increase your lifetime value?

Basics of Investing

Most 401K funds, as well as IRA, Roth IRA and your non-retirement investments are in the stock market. If your exposure is limited to your 401k choices, you may not have any education on other potential choices. Most people have not taken the time or interest to sort through the maze of options. There are many paths to learning about investments. Give yourself the time and patience to approach the process step by step.

1. Evaluate your interest and goals. Do you currently have funds available to invest? If you have time and patience, you can begin with only a few thousand dollars. If you have no personal interest and funds, you may wish to develop skills or start a business.
2. Learn the basics and use available resources.
3. Robo-advisor services are for those new to investing, having smaller portfolios. You can find reviews and minimum investment requirements with an internet search for "Best Robo-Advisors." These services can be an easy way to learn the basics.
4. When you have a $100,000 or more portfolio, you may consider a personal advisor to review your financial objectives and risk tolerance. Always investigate underlying costs for advice and trades so that you do not get surprised by hidden fees.
5. If you choose a brokerage account, do your homework. Ask others for recommendations and read reviews. Read agreements carefully to understand fees and ask questions. Feel comfortable with the people who assist you. Do not settle if you feel intimidated or frustrated. There are many quality people in the financial industry to support you
6. Invest for the long term. Investors can expect a positive return over 10-20 years. Along the way, your

investment values could also drop. The market is volatile. If you review a chart of the market from 1900 until today, you will see jagged lines which start at the lower left and take a circuitous route to the upper right where we are today. Over 120 years, the market has gone up. Conversely, you will also find periods of five to ten years where the numbers trended down.

7. Evaluate your risk tolerance. Can you experience losses without panic? Do you have both the available time and the patience to wait out a downturn? Often those who feel euphoric when their holding goes up feel a sense of despair when they go down. How do you respond?

Whom Do You Trust?

As your savings grow, you will find many investment advisors courting you to manage your account. The issue of trust is paramount. Some people avoid this issue by choosing stocks by themselves. Those who do this admit that it is time-consuming to do the research. You might love the challenge of handling your investments, and you could be lucky. Or monitoring your portfolio may be a burdensome chore in which you get failing grades. As you approach retirement, mistakes hurt significantly more, and many people decide to utilize a professional investment manager. Choose carefully and take heed of subtle danger signs.

One Hollywood film producer named Gina had been saving since she was young. By age 55, she had accumulated enough money to consider early retirement. Gina's mother was in her early seventies, and after her husband died, she sought help to manage her retirement funds. She felt safe placing her investments in the care of the family accountant. Gina's mom had been getting regular typed reports showing a consistent increase in her holdings, regardless of downturns in the market, and she felt very confident about the choices. As a result, her mother encouraged Gina to move her retirement funds to the care of the family accountant.

For the first year after the move, everything looked fine. Her mother was getting checks regularly, and the written reports showed Gina's investments thriving. Then problems popped up. Gina's mother complained that her statements were not coming regularly. Gina got suspicious and started making phone calls to confirm her investments. There was no record of them. The ruse fell apart quickly when the accountant left without a forwarding address. Gina reported the theft and engaged the FBI.

The accountant was caught, prosecuted, and jailed for pocketing and spending the money in her care. With their funds gone, Gina and her mother moved in together. They had no recourse because their accountant was not insured. Gina gave up all hopes of early retirement and set out to rebuild a retirement nest egg while also supporting her mother.

Gina and her mother overlooked some basics. Most accountants have no training in securities. Before selecting either a financial planner or an investment adviser, check their licensing. Go to https://adviserinfo.sec.gov/ You may enter the adviser's name, location, and company. You will receive a history of where that person has worked, as well as any complaints against them. If you see a complaint, that does not mean the person is guilty. The SEC registers all complaints, even if the adviser is not responsible. However, you may request an explanation, and a long series of complaints should raise concerns.

Gina and her mother got only printed reports. Documents are easy to fabricate. Most investment companies today have secure portals which provide real-time status of your accounts. You can confirm any changes in your account instantly and have secure communication with your adviser. Be cautious of any lack of privacy or security. Insist on having electronic access, which you can verify at any time.

Some people like to avoid large investment firms, feeling that a small account would be overlooked. However, major companies are under consistent scrutiny by the Securities and Exchange Commission (SEC). Their advisers must carry Errors and Omissions Insurance and provide documentation for all actions. This extra level of protection helps eliminate the potential for fraud and mistakes. Larger companies can also reimburse clients for fraud or errors. Gina and her mother had no access to funds for reimbursement.

The last part of this chapter is a short introduction to financial topics essential to women in mid-life. We do not recommend any products. We do not know you, your financial background, or your goals and dreams. However, some products have an expiration date, and if you wait too long, you may be ineligible for them. As we go through each section, take notes of any topics that you would like to explore in more depth.

Tax Impact on Retirement

Taxes have a significant impact on your retirement. Let's

make a simple comparison of the taxable and non-taxable value of $100:

- $100 taxable income at 20% is $80 of spendable income.
- $100 non-taxable income is $100 of spendable income.

In other words, $80k of NON-taxable income is equivalent to $100k taxable income.

Your 401K, IRA, and pensions are **qualified tax-deferred plans**. During your working years, you did not pay taxes on the income you deposited into these plans. As these investments grew, you did not pay taxes on the gains. In retirement, you pay income taxes on the funds you withdraw.

Your Roth IRA or Roth 401K are qualified plans. However, you paid tax BEFORE depositing funds. These funds also grow tax-free. The difference is that withdrawals are **non-taxable!**

Non-qualified investments, such as stock holdings, have different tax rules. At the end of each year, you determine your gains and losses. You owe tax on your net profit yearly. Take time to understand these rules and their impact on your retirement funds.

To determine your retirement needs, you must estimate your monthly and annual spending. Begin with a report on what you are currently spending. Then evaluate changes due to retirement. Perhaps some clothing and transportation costs will go down. However, establish a set aside for taxes based upon your income source. With the distinction between taxable and non-taxable investments in mind, let's review some additional options people consider for retirement.

Funding Your Retirement

As you approach retirement, you will develop a strategy for income from:

- Social Security
- Pensions
- 401K and Roth 401K
- IRA and Roth IRA
- Other income sources

Tax considerations will impact the amount you need. If you have access to both taxable and non-taxable income, you are in an excellent position to maximize your spendable revenue. Let's consider how this strategy works.

You are familiar with the basics of investing. The value will fluctuate year-to-year when you invest in the market, stocks/bonds/mutual funds, etc. Over a more extended time, the market has gone up, which is a good investment for retirement. When you invest for 20 years or more, your investment is likely to grow.

When you retire, you depend upon a flow of income, and downturns can feel devastating. Remember the couple that retired in 2001 and watched their retirement nest egg shrink by half? They chose to cut other expenses and change their plans because they knew that they were likely to regain their losses if they could avoid withdrawals and leave their investments for several years. Of course if they withdrew their funds, their retirement income would be gone.

Are you wondering how you will manage your living expenses during a financial downturn? You have several choices. You can trim your spending, go back to work, or utilize a strategy with tax-free money that we will review now.

The idea is simple. When your investment balance has gone down at the end of the year, pull sufficient tax-free funds to pay your expenses so that your investments can recover before you resume withdrawals from your 401K or IRA.

Of course, you must have tax-free income available. Roth programs offer tax-free savings. Many people overlook another option.

Tax-Free Income Source

Life insurance is what many people consider "death insurance" because a life insurance policy provides cash to your named beneficiaries upon your death. Life insurance can give security to a growing family, knowing there are sufficient funds to raise children if one or both of their parents die prematurely. Few people realize that permanent life insurance can also offer tax-free benefits to stretch your retirement income, and some policies also provide money for long-term care.

Many families utilize life insurance as a tool in their estate planning. It can provide tax-free money to beneficiaries, funds for a succession plan, charitable donations, equalizing inheritance for family members, and more. Life insurance can be a valuable tool if you spend the time to understand your options AND you are insurable. Sadly, I often get calls from people who are not eligible for a policy due to their health and age. The best time to learn about it is when you are young, and the truth is that you will never be more youthful than you are today!

There are two major categories of life insurance: temporary and permanent. Temporary insurance is called Term Insurance. Like your auto or home insurance, you choose the amount of insurance and the length of coverage. Life insurance payments, called premiums, are non-refundable, and your beneficiaries receive the death payment if you die while the policy is in force. Premiums are low while you are young and healthy. As you age, premiums increase. Many companies do not write term insurance over a certain age. There are almost no companies that offer term life insurance to those over age 85.

Permanent life insurance is non-cancellable for life, as long as premiums are maintained. Permanent life insurance can pay dividends, annual payments to policyholders based upon the insurance company's profitability. These are similar to corporate dividends paid to stockholders. Mutual insurance companies do not have stockholders and consider their policyholders to be the owners of the company. They typically pay higher dividends to policyholders than insurance companies that issue stock and report to stockholders. Dividends are announced annually by the insurance company. Current dividends in 2022 are approximately 6% per year. As a point of comparison, high-paying savings accounts are currently paying 0.30% interest.

As the cash value in a permanent life insurance policy grows, it is tax advantaged. Cash value in your permanent life insurance policy may be used for any purpose because it is your money. You may access your cash value either as a loan or a withdrawal. Withdrawals from your cash value may be taxable, so some experts recommend borrowing the cash value from your account. You may have to pay interest on your borrowed money. However, that may be good news if you are paying the interest to yourself! An additional benefit is that you do not need to repay the money you borrowed. You have a life insurance policy that guarantees the note. At the insured's death, the life insurance policy eliminates any outstanding loan balance, reducing the settlement amount paid to your beneficiaries. You decide whether to repay your cash value loans based upon your specific needs!

If you plan to take retirement income from your 401K or private investments, the cash value in your permanent life insurance policy provides a valuable alternative to stretch your funds. Market-based returns are volatile, and during retirement, you need funds annually. Withdrawals in a down year leave you with much lower balances for future growth.

If you have cash value in a life insurance policy, you can withdraw tax-advantaged money from your life insurance policy rather than selling stocks. By maintaining your invested funds, your investments have time to rebound. This bear market strategy is helpful for professionals and business owners but requires planning. The details of your assets, health, and age will impact the result. When you work with a licensed professional specializing in retirement strategies, you get a detailed plan that works for you.

Long Term Care Insurance

Life insurance can also provide long-term care funding with a long-term care rider or accumulated cash value. Current estimates are that 50% of people over 65 will need long-term care for some period of their life. Women need assistance longer than men. Since women frequently outlive men, it is vital to have a plan. Long-term care assistance can cost $6,000 to $10,000 per month, either at home or facility. Medicare does not cover this expense. Some states have programs that assist people of low income, but not all. Planning is more important for women because statistically, women outlive men by five years. Often one spouse will care for the other. But what happens to the surviving spouse?

Long-term care is sometimes confused with senior living facilities. Long-term care insurance coverage is activated when an individual requires assistance with two or more of the following activities of daily life: eating, bathing, toileting, dressing, transferring, and continence. Cognitive disorders like dementia and Alzheimer's also qualify one for long-term care assistance. Currently, about 65% of the aging will need long-term care. One-third of today's 65-year-olds will never need long-term care, yet approximately 20% will need it for five years or more. A long-term care rider on a life insurance policy can provide peace of mind. And those who never need long-term care will have access to the cash value and the death benefit for beneficiaries. A long-term care insurance rider provides value regardless of whether you require assisted care.

Some states provide long-term care assistance for those who cannot afford it based on their income and assets. Take time to understand the rules in your state and plan accordingly. Moving assets to your children to qualify can trigger penalties based upon timing.

I regularly get long-term care insurance inquiries from

people in their seventies. Unfortunately, they are ineligible due to age or health. The best time to consider long-term care coverage is before age 65 when you are in good health. Almost 30% of long-term care applications are declined for underlying medical conditions.

Life insurance with a long-term care rider is valuable to single women. One client purchased a life insurance policy with a long-term care rider to cover her needs. Although she has no children, she wants to leave a significant gift to a charitable foundation. Her policy gives her peace of mind for her future and provides a growing legacy for her charitable foundation.

The unique characteristics of a life insurance policy make it ideal for a variety of uses:

- **Financial foundation for children.** Often, parents or grandparents purchase permanent life insurance policies for their children or grandchildren. Grandparents might fully pay this policy over ten to twenty years. The cash value could then be available for college expenses, buying their first home, or retirement. It is a lifetime gift, and a relatively small contribution can significantly affect a child's future. Also, the child may have this policy for life, even if their insurability changes.
- **Protection combined with savings.** Young couples often purchase insurance to protect their new family. Some people buy a term policy because it is less expensive. If their budget allows, a permanent policy might enable them to set aside funds for goals like a

down payment on a new home, funding to start a business, a child's college, or retirement.

Biases against permanent life insurance began decades ago. In the 1970s, A.L. Williams coined the phrase, "Buy term and invest the difference." The theory was that instead of putting $300 per month into a whole life policy, you would come out ahead if you paid $30 for a comparable term life policy and invested the difference of $270 every month. This catchy phrase is still around 50 years later. While no single solution is suitable for everyone, history has shown the fallacy in "Buy term and invest the difference."

- Those who "buy term" rarely "invest the difference." Term insurance is an excellent and affordable protection for families. Yet, the rate of savings has fallen from 12% to 3% since 1970. Many families do not even have $400 emergency savings.
- Investments are volatile. They may have a higher return over time, but they are not guaranteed. All investments are not the same. Individual choices will determine the outcome.
- Consider your financial self-discipline. Are you more likely to pay a monthly premium or make a monthly investment?
- Be aware that if you have an expired term policy and want to keep your insurance, the premium will be higher. It goes up every year by age. Be aware that the sooner you investigate life insurance, the lower the

rates. Waiting for years always increases your premiums.

Tune into your financial biases. Running comparisons based upon your situation provides a reasonable basis for a sound decision. Blindly following advice from family or friends can lead to disappointment. The world today is not the same as it was twenty years ago. Get accurate information and trust yourself. In the upcoming chapter for business owners, we will also review other benefits of life insurance.

Annuities

Running out of money is the biggest fear most people have in retirement. Very few can live on Social Security. In the movie "Nomadland," Frances McDormand plays the award-winning and heart-bending role of an older woman named Fern, who has lost her husband and doesn't have money to retire. She packs up a camper van and finds temporary jobs. Fern demonstrates determination and a will to create a life of adventure. Her creativity and hard work are admirable. Yet her life is not one that most of us would choose.

What would you do if you ran out of money? It can be a reality.Social Security and pensions provide lifelong income, yet your 401K, investments, real estate, and other retirement income sources could run out. There is another source for lifetime income that you might have overlooked. Have you heard about an annuity with a guaranteed lifetime withdrawal benefit?

An annuity is a contract between an individual (or couple) and a life insurance company. You may purchase an annuity with retirement savings or with payments over time. The money in an annuity grows tax deferred. You have control over your money, but there are penalties for more than 10% withdrawals in the first few years. An annuity is for funds that you do not anticipate using in the next few years.

Annuities can be part of a diversified retirement portfolio because they protect you from downturns in the market. They provide protected lifetime income that few other financial products offer.

Some annuities are optimized to provide long-term care coverage, which offers double to triple times the purchase price of the annuity. These are designed only for those who are healthy and under age 65. Even if you never need long-term care coverage, you have life insurance, AND access to your annuity funds. They offer peace of mind against the cost of long-term care, along with flexibility for the future. Consider a long-term care solution in your fifties or no later than age 65. Even younger adults are denied coverage when they have underlying health issues. If you are 50 and in good health, it is an excellent time to consider long-term care options with life insurance or annuities.

Some people have biases against annuities. One couple inherited an annuity from her parents. She only had access to a monthly distribution, and she wanted the total amount for real-estate investing. She blamed annuities for the restriction. The reality is that her mother chose this method of estate distribution. Some parents restrict the flow of money to prevent their children from overspending. The insurance company must follow the instructions given by the original owner. An annuity is a financial tool. It can provide lifetime income or distribute your inheritance based on your instructions.

Anna and Bill had a different experience. The year they planned to retire, they watched half of their retirement savings vanish in a down market. They managed to cut expenses, rent out their house, and travel in a van for more than a year until the value of their retirement savings rebounded. They wanted to avoid problems in the future. They purchased a series of annuities that began in 7-year intervals. Their plan enabled a guaranteed income with increases for inflation every seven years. Those who like annuities appreciate the simplicity. There is no need to monitor investments or real estate. They simply collect checks!

Annuities offer guarantees. As a fiscally conservative tool, they are best for those close to retirement. If you have ten to twenty years before retiring, you have time to consider invest-ments with a higher return. An annuity is a tool. When you understand how it works, you can determine whether it is worthwhile in your situation.

Real Estate

Many people swear that real estate is the best investment for long-term gains. One of the factors that make real estate attractive is leverage. You can purchase a rental home with a 20% down payment and sometimes less. Then you can rent it out to cover the mortgage. The current national appreciation rate for homes is 3.5 to 3.8 percent per year. If all goes according to plan, your renter pays your mortgage, the house appreciates, the rents go up, and you have an ongoing cash flow. This scenario gives you the cash to retire or sell the house for a profit if you need extra money. What could be wrong with this?

We are not in a position to give you advice on individual real-estate deals. Even bulletproof agreements have fallen apart while unlikely buildings might become cash cows. We want to offer a few "thinking points" to consider along the way.

Raw land can provide a reasonable ROI. But it can also be a trap for the inexperienced. Beware of promises of future development. One gentleman bought a lot in Colorado, where the neighborhood already had streets and plumbing available. He purchased the lot for $7,000. Twenty years later, after a divorce, he decided to sell the lot. He received $6500 after sales commissions. The development had stalled with only a handful of homes completed. Do your research.

Single-family home rentals provide monthly income to retire a mortgage and pay for upkeep and repairs. Remember to allow for vacancies in your calculations. High-priced areas, like California, offer significant appreciation but frequently run cash-flow negative, which means that you will pay out of pocket for expenses not covered by rental income. The return comes when you sell the property in the future.

If you are the property manager, repairs and upkeep become your responsibility. If you hire someone, do your homework. A property manager can make or break your experience. Monitor your renters. Bad renters might ruin the property, and lack of regular maintenance can result in high and unanticipated costs.

Insure your property against losses and protect both the renter and you. Liability insurance is a must for a property owner. Speak to a lawyer who can advise you about creating an

LLC for real estate ownership and personal trusts to protect you from major losses through lawsuits.

Multi-unit rental properties are valued differently from single-family homes. Calculate apartment building value by determining the income it generates after maintenance and repair costs. How much revenue does it generate relative to the cost of operation? What is the current condition? Are repairs required? What is the occupancy rate?

Commercial buildings and apartments are valued based upon their profitability. Successful owners weigh the cost of upkeep and improvements relative to increased rent potential.

Experienced multi-unit building owners create well-run management systems. Rentals might be a good retirement income if you can operate multi-unit buildings profitably without your personal time and effort.

Many people love real estate investing. They enjoy the experience, and the value of their properties increases. I know other friends who purchased homes out of state, thinking that a property manager would give them turn-key success. One friend had two inattentive property managers, a house that needed pricey mold remediation, and high vacancy rates. She sold three years later at a 50% loss. Her out-of-state real estate purchase was a learning experience.

Consider how taxes will impact you. Real estate income from rents is taxable annually after you subtract your costs. An increase in your equity is not taxable until you sell the property. Learning the tax rules that apply in the state where you own real estate will be necessary to your retirement and estate planning. If you have purchased rental real estate with your Roth IRA funds, your rents are not taxable income! And your capital gains are also tax-free. However, if you sell property purchased with a Roth IRA at a loss, you may not deduct the loss from your taxes. So, choose wisely.

What Is Right for You?

In mid-life, it is vital to examine your attitudes toward money. Look at your current habits and ask yourself where they will lead you in the next 30 years. If you have made financial mistakes, be kind to yourself. You are not alone. We learn through our mistakes. Mistakes provide unforgettable lessons. Be humble. Celebrate your wins and be open to learning from others.

As I turned 50, I felt young and vital. Planning for retirement seemed like a task for the future. Yet, my optimistic attitude did not alter the law of compound interest. Money needs time to grow. If you don't set aside money for the future, you could be relying on a winning lottery ticket to fund your retirement.

As you consider your choices for retirement savings, you must place the hard-earned fruits of your life work in the hands of another. Saving money and investing requires trust and faith. It is prudent to keep at least seven years of your annual salary for retirement. That is a large sum of money which may represent almost a decade of your work life. Where are you now? The average 50-year-old in the United States has a savings of $150,000. What is your savings goal by 65 or 70 for retirement? And where will you save this money?

I found myself far short of my retirement savings goals when I turned 50. A highly respected friend approached me with an opportunity. He would pay me 4% per month on a loan of $100,000 and repay me in 6 months to a year. I had never considered this kind of private investment. But I trusted my friend, and it seemed like a great way to accelerate my savings growth. It took me a week to get my retirement funds released. I paid the penalties and taxes to release the money. I was looking forward to having $125,000 in 6 months and enjoying my good fortune working with this friend.

What I had provided was a hard money loan with no guarantees. My friend never got the funds he was expecting. His business fell apart, and no one recovered their funds. He lost his home while I lost my retirement savings. This lose-lose deal had lessons for each of us. The money I accumulated over seven years vanished without recourse. In retrospect, I could have asked better questions to evaluate my risk. Most investments offer better guarantees than my all-or-nothing choice. I opened myself to risk at a time in my life when prudence was preferable. When deciding what to do with money, be your own best friend. Ask questions, look at alternatives.

Real stories provide lessons through the experience of others. The women in the following examples are intelligent, knowledgeable professionals. Each of them has built companies, taken care of their families, and created wonderful lives. Money mistakes happen to everyone.

Mary inherited $400,000 from her mother. Sarah, one of her best friends, formed a limited partnership to build a housing development and invited Mary to invest. Mary quickly jumped at the opportunity to double or triple her investment and added funds from her savings. She invested a total of $863,000. Because she trusted Sarah, Mary didn't take time to understand the workings of a limited partnership. Sarah and a builder were the General Partners. Mary was a limited partner and was not entitled to timely updates and reports on the finances. The project failed after the builder left the program taking payment in full for his participation. Sarah, as the lone General Partner, was left handling the mess. Mary and other investors did not receive advance notice until the total investment was gone and the project bankrupt.

Mary felt angry and betrayed, and they did not speak. Years later, they reconnected briefly. Sarah sent a check for $23,000 in partial reparation and told Mary that she would find a way to repay her. These women were both vulnerable due to unasked questions and undefined risks. Mary lost a significant investment to a trusted friend, while Sarah banked her future on this business deal, losing not only the project but her home, assets, friends, and reputation.

Losing money hurts your pride and your future while losing trust in others hurts your soul. How can we make better choices? What are the questions to ask? While there are no simple rules for guidance, we CAN ask better questions. Keep exploring until you fully understand both the risk and the reward and any additional investment of time or money along the way. We all perk up our ears when someone has a lucrative investment. Be selective about sources of information. Ask questions, and then ask more questions. Seek knowledgeable expertise from a variety of sources and expand beyond Google to include professionals and experts. Avoid any pressure to make instant decisions.

Ask yourself who you trust. Even good people make mistakes. Investigate before you invest. Talk to experts and search their credentials. You can get details about any agent's insurance or securities licenses. Research your investments. Even good friends and respected professionals make mistakes. Your investments should make sense to you.

KEYS FOR REFLECTION:

Review your thoughts and feelings about investing.

- What have you learned that you want to put into practice?
- What financial topics do you want to explore? By when?
- What is your current financial position?
- What will you change to make life more financially secure in your future?
- What types of investments interest you?
- How can you start saving NOW for your future?

Chapter Eleven

THE EMOTIONS OF MONEY

"Wealth is the ability to fully experience life."
~Henry David Thoreau

IN THE PAST FEW CHAPTERS, we have reviewed some financial vehicles for building wealth for retirement. As you read those details, what did you feel? You might have been curious to read something new, or bored and thinking, "I already know that" or felt distracted and set the book down to attend to something else. Be honest with yourself. What were you thinking and feeling?

You may have heard the phrase, "How you do one thing is how you do everything." I guarantee that sentiment applies here. Money and finances are emotional triggers. As you consider your future, your emotion is a critical component. Our next step is to examine your model of reality and your habits.

Then we will connect your important life goals with your money sense.

If the last chapters were complicated and you found yourself distracted and skipping pages, you are not alone. Money is a profound source of emotion that can launch feelings of shame, incompetence, and even a desire to nap or distract yourself. Of course, money can make you feel fabulous, and we all value the beautiful things it can provide. However, few people have arrived at a state of being "profoundly sufficient," which is a phrase from Lynne Twist's book *The Soul of Money*. The feeling of "profoundly sufficiency" arises when you have enough money for what is truly important to you. You may have felt this at certain times in your life. Perhaps you just purchased a new home and felt satisfied that you have a new home and a reasonable monthly payment. Or maybe you went on a grocery trip and had more than enough to feed your family for the next week. For most of us, sufficiency is transient.

As we consider funding the remainder of our lives, the stakes are high. The true meaning of "profound sufficiency" applies to retirement savings. Having enough to live in our chosen comfort level for an unknown number of years is the goal. We cannot satisfy this need with momentary satisfaction. Is it any wonder that we may find ourselves distracted and longing to change the subject?

Distraction is a standard method of avoiding underlying internal conflict. This discussion of money leads to a profoundly spiritual and metaphysical discussion of life vision and life purpose. By mid-life, we have experienced love, success, and failure. We regret the roads not taken. Now is the time to bubble these feelings into conscious awareness.

Money is a form of energy. We create money in our life through our work and talents. Life becomes easy when our energy aligns with our soul wishes. In other words, when we are happy and feel productive and appreciated, we are likely to create more money. Quite simply, our feelings impact our finances. The profound question arises, "What is the source of our feelings about ourselves and money?"

Model of the World

We all have our unique Model of the World, which we have developed throughout life. As we observe parents, teachers, and friends who share their beliefs, habits, and attitudes, we create a personal model to guide our actions. This individual model generates both successes and failures. Your beliefs and your actions shape the life you have made. Let's take a few minutes to explore some of your attitudes toward money and success. Ask yourself the following questions:

- Do you think of money as good or bad?
- In what way is money good?
- In what way is money bad?
- When you have personally saved and accumulated money, how do you feel about it?

Our model informs our attitudes toward both work and enjoyment. The founder of MindValley.com, Vishen Lakiani, shared how his unconscious model impacted him. After the birth of his first child, Vishen shortened his workday to spend time raising his new son. Despite having eighteen employees in his growing company, Vishen saw his profits plummet within a few short months. During this time, Vishen also studied with personal development and coaching masters who urged him to examine his beliefs. He had an AHA moment while remembering an incident when he was very young. His father came home from work and collapsed on the floor from exhaustion. Vishen internalized the scene, accepting that he must WORK HARD for money. He recognized that by taking time away from his business, he had betrayed this unwritten rule. His self-limiting belief sabotaged his ongoing success. This AHA moment allowed Vishen to shift his emotional response and make changes.

Working together with his team, he became more efficient. They initiated new campaigns, and within six months, his company went from losing $20K per month to profiting an additional million dollars by the end of the year. Vishen continued to spend time with his family and attributes the difference to his changed mindset. I suspect that changing his mindset was only a first step. He had a quality team of employees who all contributed.

How might your mindset be impacting your finances? Does this story have any similarities in your life? Why not take a moment to journal your thoughts or stories? Be willing to write about whatever comes up for you, even if you do not yet see a link. Your intuition may guide you to memories that are ripe for exploration.

Habits and Routines

Our routines define our days and shape our environment.

Personal habits save time because we avoid over-thinking repetitive actions that serve us. We recognize that eating and exercise routines determine our health while our saving and investing strategies build our financial health. Yet, we can also be blind to the connection between our habits and beliefs.

Years ago, I had a business coaching client named Nancy, who stumbled upon a connection between her spending habits and her business success. Nancy started a new online business, meticulously following a roadmap for growth and success. One of the recommended strategies was to allocate income to various areas. Nancy was proudly precise in dividing her income for necessities, immediate savings, long-term savings, education, and fun. After several months, I noticed that Nancy's fun money continued to grow, unspent. I asked if she was saving for a special event. Sheepishly, Nancy told me that she felt uncomfortable spending this money. It didn't feel right to her to "waste" money on her fun!

During this time, Nancy's business was not growing. She was doing the work, but lacked a personal connection. She wasn't engaged in life – either spending her fun money or enjoying her business. The link between fun and success came into focus. As a child, Nancy's parents said that she could only have necessities. It was a dour life with little fun. Nancy longed for more as an adult yet wasn't convinced she deserved it. Nancy committed to spending some fun money within the week. First, she allocated $10 for ice cream with a friend. Next, she planned a family vacation. It was an economical camping trip, but the change of pace and focus on the fun was transformational.

Nancy learned to enjoy life, even in her business. Nancy

hadn't expected these small changes to make much difference, but to her surprise, her online business began to grow. She found ways to enjoy her daily routine. She found creativity in designing advertisements and new friends who were also business owners.

Locating and shifting unconscious drivers can make a profound difference, although it often requires one-to-one coaching. Expanding your imagination and vision can open new vistas and self-discovery. Our next step is to dig for the fun in YOUR life. As you are creating your roadmap for the future, I recommend the following exercise.

Your Top 100

True wealth comes from living your best life. Many people never explore the possibilities. Challenge yourself by creating your list of "100 Things to Do in This Lifetime." You can call it your "bucket list" or your "soul wishes." The steps are simple:

- Get a notebook that you will use now and keep for the future.
- Put a title at the top of the page called "Top 100" and the date.
- Number each line on the page from 1 to 100.
- Set a timer for 20 minutes.
- Fill each line with something you would like to do, have, or be.

You can list significant goals, like buying a beach condo or traveling the world for a year. List simple things like spending an evening listening to music with girlfriends or organizing your closet. Drop the urge to prioritize. The list of 100 is a challenge that forces you to dive into your heartfelt secrets. The act of writing them out will surprise you as you uncover dreams you may have forgotten. Keep your pen moving. Imagine a genie granting you every wish, but you only get those written on the page before the timer rings. Keep asking, "What makes me happy?" My list has "a clean house" right next to "$5 Million in savings."

After twenty minutes, take a deep breath and review your list. Do you find recurring themes? What surprises you? Did you get to 100, or is there room for more? The good news is that you create the rules. You might even continue adding to your list as you get inspiration. Make this your happy list. Sticking to the 20-minute timeframe has several advantages:

- The process will not become an overwhelming task. Set your timer to stop in 20 minutes. You CAN afford 20 minutes to design your future, even with a busy, stressful life. You will benefit from this break if you have significant stress.
- The short timeframe can stop you from over-analyzing. If you have an idea, write it down. You are filling a shopping basket with all you might ever want. Avoid analysis-paralysis. You are not prioritizing. Write now and review later!
- Do your best to fill the page in 20 minutes. There is no limit. If you write fast, you have permission to exceed 100 dreams. Make it a game and go to town!

When finished, share your list with your partner or a friend. Calendar some wishes to enjoy this year and acknowledge your unique life vision. If you have available numbers, you can also add satisfying things that are already in your life. For example, I love growing orchids in my kitchen window. Adding orchids to my list makes me grateful for a piece of my perfect life that is already here! Appreciation and gratitude increase wealth. This exercise brings a deeper understanding of yourself. To deepen your relationship with your partner, do the activity together and compare your results. You may uncover visions to create as a couple.

Money is so much more than math. Your list of 100 can give you some specific targets for living well:

- Circle the activities or accomplishments that are most important, keeping the total to about ten. Estimate the cost of each item beyond your average living expense.
- Calculate the impact of inflation on your living expenses by increasing your current total by 2% a year which corresponds to the inflation target of the FED. For example, if your monthly expense were $100 at age 65, the acceleration might look like this:
- $100 at age 65
- $122 at age 75
- $149 at age 85
- $181 at age 95
- $221 at age 105

It may be apparent that a long life can get expensive! The 50-year span outlined above is very conservative.

As we consider how to create money for life, recognize that we are navigating without a compass. If you find yourself worrying, stop and think of another path. If you and I were at sea without a compass, we would quickly learn that all mind chatter is meaningless. Instead, we could study our surroundings. Where is the sun rising and setting? This knowledge would allow us to identify east and west. What is on the horizon? A speck in the distance could provide a clue or a new course direction. A distant sky might warn of a coming storm, allowing time to prepare. Even without a guidebook, you find your way through life by the same process.

The first step is to map out your current position:

1. Determining your net worth is crucial because it allows you to see where you are storing financial value.
2. Inventory your skills, and talents which are your source of prosperity.
3. Next, list your innate gifts. It is easy to disregard those easy talents for us, although they may be the source of hidden treasure!

Explore aspects of your life that you want to shift. By continuing to grow and explore, you keep the adventure in your life. You are responsible for creating your life as long as you breathe.

1. Review your list of 100 for repeating themes. Are you

finding simple adjustments to your current life? Or are you discovering a sharp change of direction?

2. Journal the life goals and experiences which light you up. Imagine making changes. What would you want to do first? Who would support your decision and root for your success? Who might discourage you and insist that you continue as you are?

3. Consciously create your list of life goals with an awareness of your fulfillment as well as potential obstacles.

4. Watch your horizon for insight and inspiration as you steer your energies toward your goals. Learn every moment by staying alert and awake, by living consciously and intentionally.

Refresh yourself by enjoying the beauty and any small surprises along the way. Daily experience increases your wisdom. Bring the facts of your life together with your desired future.

Recognizing your current financial position provides you with today's starting point, and an understanding of your financial choices will assist you in finding your economic way. None of these will give you all the answers. The sailor must make a series of choices and enjoy the ride, and I recommend that you do the same.

As you gain this clarity, watch out for the hidden whirlpools that take you off course and scramble your compass. Each of us brings biases to our understanding of money. In the book *The Psychology of Money*, author Morgan Housel shares the 2006 research of economists covering 50 years of the Consumer

Finance Survey. The study found that while most people can identify their goals and the characteristics of the investment options available to them, they will rarely follow a recommended path. Instead, they follow self-guidance created during their youth with little objective understanding. In other words, they know what professionals would recommend, but they stubbornly do it their way. The question is, WHY?

Two of the studies in Morgan Housel's book give us insight. We have a monetary history that sways our judgment based upon when we were born. One study measured growth in the stock market for those born in two different time frames: 1950 and 1970. Those born in 1950 saw a flat stock market between the ages of 13 and 30. Those born in 1970 saw the market rise to over nine times the initial value in their teens and twenties. You would understand that those born in 1970 might have a much higher expectation of earnings from stock investments than those born in 1950.

A second study in *The Psychology of Money* evaluated the impact of inflation. The first group, born in 1960, saw prices more than double between age 13 and 30. Imagine having your first job as prices continually rose. The second group, born 30 years later in 1990, saw only gradual inflation creep in their youth. These young people experienced consistent prices. How might your inflation concerns differ depending upon your experience?

It may help to acknowledge your financial biases. However, friends with the same experience are likely to support your views. Each of us brings our life experiences to our choices today. What details stick with you? Was it success or struggle that impacts you today?

Can you relate to working hours past exhaustion and passing up events or vacations because it wasn't in the budget? Have you, like me, worried about how to pay for health insurance, replacement tires, or a night out with friends? I admit to being bankrupt more than once.

My first bankruptcy was my father's. The year before I started high school, my father purchased a Buick dealership in Southern California. The economy was diving into a recession which most economists called a "rolling adjustment." It impacted several major industries, most notably automobiles. My dad had been so proud to show off "Dick Herrick Buick" on Pacific Boulevard. I thought our family had arrived when I sat on the new leather sofa in his office and walked into his private bathroom. Yet within a year, everything changed. Cars were not selling anywhere. Buicks didn't sell. The leather sofa came home to our house, and the dealership closed.

My mother was an expert at stretching the food budget. We didn't buy anything unless it was necessary. My brothers and sisters were much younger and didn't seem to notice. Mom brought home large refrigerator and washing machine boxes, and the younger children created forts and clubhouses. They enjoyed the bliss of children. And we survived.

My dad had a friend in the insurance industry who approached him with a business idea. Together they created insurance packages designed for automobile dealerships. The two friends birthed a successful business. When my dad was ready to retire, he sold the rights of his proprietary package to Farmers Insurance Company.

My story is not unusual. Most successes had failures along the way. One personal development guru claimed that bankruptcy was a rite of passage to great success. While I am not willing to make that assertion, I do know that failure is not fatal. Think of your upbringing. How did money impact your life? What were the good times? Can you recall happiness and joy? What were the challenging times? How did you cope? What impact did money have on your life? Did it inspire you? Or did it disappoint you and dash your hopes? While I love marketing images of good times with plenty of money, that was not my reality. I lived the truth that money doesn't dictate happiness, while lack of money won't prevent it. Sharing half a sandwich with a friend can be a happy time, whether you are the giver or recipient. Money is something else entirely.

KEYS FOR REFLECTION:

1. How does money impact your life?
2. What are your financial weaknesses?
3. What are your financial strengths?
4. How much monthly income will provide you with profound sufficiency?
5. List the changes you want to make in your finances

   - What are your priorities?
   - What is your timeframe?
   - How will you hold yourself accountable?

Chapter Twelve

SMALL BUSINESS OWNER RETIREMENT

en·tre·pre·neur

A person who organizes and operates a business or businesses, taking on greater than normal financial risks in order to do so.

THIS CHAPTER IS NOT for everyone but essential for some. If you currently have a small business, please read this. If you consider starting a business to beef up your retirement income, this chapter is essential—the fate of the small business owner tugs at my soul. I regularly speak with business owners who have little or nothing in retirement savings. Often, they don't even have much Social Security. As a result, many of them simply continue to work. You might ask, "What happened?

Didn't they follow the American dream?" Each story is unique, yet there are some identifiable trends.

My father was a small business owner. He owned a Buick dealership which bankrupted as I was entering high school. With five children at home and one on the way, my dad got busy. He partnered with a friend in the insurance industry to create a unique offering for automobile dealers. When Dad was ready to retire, he had a marketable offering and sold his program rights to Farmer's Insurance. Unfortunately, the majority of small business owners are not so lucky.

A small business has 500 or fewer employees. The United States has over 30 million small businesses based on current estimates. Companies with fewer than 100 employees account for 98%, while 89% have fewer than 20 employees.

Small businesses in the United States are responsible for 1.5 million or 64% of the new jobs created annually. As job losses mounted during 2020, new business applications grew. By September 2020, requests for new EINs were at 3.2 million compared to 2.7 million in 2019. Many people felt that this was the right time to go into business for themselves. The verdict is out on their success.

As you explore your future funding, you may need more money. Are you asking yourself if starting your own business is a good idea? Personal responsibility for your future can feel liberating yet stepping into a new venture without prior experience is both exciting and frightening.

Many people have learned how to use technology more efficiently. You can sell almost anything online, and videoconferencing connects the world. New ideas blossom with ease in this environment.

Yet, the US Bureau of Labor Statistics may give you a reason to pause. Approximately 20% of new businesses fail during the first two years, while 45% fail in the first five years and 65% during the first ten years. Only 25% of new businesses make it to fifteen years or more.

There is more bad news about retirement for business owners. Unfortunately, many don't plan. It can take years to prepare for a profitable business sale. There must be systems in place for the business to remain profitable. And the business owner must have a clear path to replace business income with retirement income.

What I have observed is that small financial choices accumulate over time to sabotage a retirement plan. Could this happen to you? Ask yourself the following questions:

- Have you contributed to FICA to provide for your Social Security?
- Have you created an IRA, SEP IRA, or company retirement plan?
- Have you contributed to a retirement plan regularly?
- Do you have a succession plan?
- Have you set up buy-out agreements with partners for potential death or disability? Have you funded the plan?
- Have you determined the value of your company?

Business owners sometimes develop a myopic focus on lowering income taxes. Rather than paying income and FICA taxes, they choose to beef up business deductions by purchasing a new car or investing in training courses that provide business deductions. In doing this, they rob themselves of future retirement. They are proud of avoiding taxes yet damage their retirement potential in the process. A financial support team can round out your business understanding. Be sure to include people with varied expertise who can widen your monetary knowledge.

If you have realized that you need additional retirement income, give yourself the time to succeed. You CAN create a business that provides the income you need, but you need time, knowledge, and support. I believe that wise women at mid-life can change the direction of their lives and the direction of the world, and we do it one step at a time.

What Makes a Great Business?

If you want a successful business, start by enjoying what you do. Have a sense of PASSION that drives you. Be kind to yourself. Evaluate your preferences. Ask yourself, "If I could do one thing for the next ten years that would make me happy, what would that be?

Would you be writing or baking? Would you have people around? Would you speak on stage? Or do you prefer helping people? Maybe you would enjoy social media or technology? What makes you happy? Ask your close friends for ideas. Keep a journal of your thoughts. Sleep on them and see how you feel. And then continue with the next steps.

1. Identify a market need and the product or service that satisfies it.

If you want to understand your target market, watch a few episodes of "Shark Tank." Every pitch defines the problem that their product or service solves. You will see both winners and losers. Notice how the sharks ask pointed questions and give reasons for their offers and declines. To define your market, you need your ideal client's age, gender, and problem. You must know where they live, how you will reach them, and what they are willing to pay. Some new entrepreneurs declare that their offer is for everyone. To a savvy investor, this is a sign that you haven't done your homework. Until you identify your market, you have not found a buyer!

2. Identify and source your capital.

It takes money to launch a business. In addition to product creation, you need funds to market and staff your offer. Companies without capital cripple their marketing, production, and growth. Consider finding investors through crowdfunding, grants, or business loans. While some people loathe all debt, there is a hidden benefit in seeking capital to start your business. A business plan is essential to get funding. Your plan requires clear communication of your ideas and accurate estimates of your expenses. The discipline of this process is invaluable. Investors will challenge what they don't understand. This process helps to refine your strategies and projections. Involving other people expands your perspective. Investors can also cheer for you and promote you. When they believe in you, they can provide the capital you need.

3. Choose the right team.

A successful business requires a balanced mix of personalities who are all working in the best role. Do you know your strengths and weaknesses? If you are active in your business, you must understand what you bring. I have worked with individuals and companies to explore their behavior styles using a DISC profile. What makes this particular profile valuable in business is the focus on observable behavior. You do not need the services of a psychologist to evaluate potential employees or partners.

The DISC profile considers two observable behaviors. The first is PACE, and the second is FOCUS.

PACE is simply one's preferred speed which is observable. Fast-paced individuals move quickly and like to get things done. Fast-paced individuals may also miss the details that a slower-paced individual would notice.

FOCUS can be primarily on people or things/data/details. Generally, sales professionals relate more to people, while technicians focus on the data and facts. There is no best way to be.

Understanding your personal preferences can clarify the skills and qualities you might want to hire for business success. For example, I am people-oriented and engaged when working with people. Simultaneously, I may skip details or be too easygoing, letting deadlines slip. I need a team member who communicates well and keeps us on schedule with urgency. I also need people who track facts to maintain quality and monitor the budget.

What do you bring to your business? What are your strengths and preferred roles? What could be missing? What kind of teammate will elevate your results?

4. Define Your Competition

Who is your competition? What is working for them? It is unlikely that you are unique. A Google search for your products or services will give you a list of companies. And even with competition, there is room for new ideas and approaches. What sets you apart?

I have faced competition in both the personal coaching and the financial sectors. There are many qualified people in those industries, and each of them could quickly satisfy my clients. Competition is everywhere. Yet, I am the only ME. You are the only YOU. Self-acceptance and generosity are the ground zero of defining your offering in very personal services. Take time to celebrate your uniqueness! Step back and evaluate your offer, using a classic approach, the SWOT analysis.

The questions below answered thoughtfully can bring clarity. Invite business associates and those you respect to participate in this analysis.

STRENGTHS: What are your special or unique advantages? Is it the product? The people? The marketing? The timing? The target market? Be effusive and complete in listing your strengths.

WEAKNESS: What could cause you to fail? Do you have the funding? The right people? Effective marketing? Do you have a clear understanding of the business? Effective systems? Reliable suppliers? Industry knowledge or advisors?

OPPORTUNITY: What growth is possible? Do you see yourself as an early adopter of a new idea? Are you introducing a high-demand product or service? What are your opportunities for expansion? Can you build a company that is ripe for a significant buyout? What makes NOW the right time for your offer?

THREATS: What could deal a fatal blow to your business? Could a change in tax or employment laws impact you? Might you lose your market if your primary supplier raised your cost of goods? Or your rent increased? Could a competitor provide a solution that is better and cheaper? What might put you out of business?

Taking the time to evaluate your competition and complete a SWOT analysis can give you a view of your business without blinders. There can be risks in your business, and if you still see the potential, you can move forward. Doing an annual SWOT analysis is a helpful way to maintain a solid and robust business.

5. Price It Right

Pricing your product is an art. Low prices could attract customers or give them the impression that you have a low-quality offering. It is worth your time to evaluate the price of competitive offers. Consider both products themselves and other possible solutions.

Let me provide an example: two business coaches may have very similar content and timing. The person considering their services also has a third option which is to do nothing. The cost of doing nothing is to continue getting the current result. If you were pricing coaching services, you do not need to price your services lower than another coach. You need to demonstrate that doing nothing has a cost much higher than your fee.

To understand pricing options, consider the entire picture. Imagine you sell tires. The person coming to you needs tires now. They can purchase from a low-cost competitor who is twelve miles away for price A. You are offering the tires for Price A + $40. You have several choices to get the sale. You could lower your price since the customer is right there. Or you might ask the customer how much it costs to drive twelve miles and spend hours waiting vs. leaving the car now and getting a courtesy ride home. Suddenly, your offer is far more appealing because it eliminates a trip, saving both time and money.

Price your product or service wisely. Research the options. Understand the contribution of a loss leader to your business bottom line. Acknowledge whether your pricing is putting you out of business. Keep abreast of changes in your industry.

6. Your Exit Plan

If you have a business and have reached age 50, it is time to decide how your business contributes to your retirement plan. Most business owners ignore this last sentence. Many will say that they don't plan to retire because they like running their business. Yet, I get calls when a business owner faces a health crisis. While they might fight and win their health challenge, the reality is chilling.

I support your option to run your business as long as you want. I believe you also deserve the opportunity to capitalize on your life's work and harvest the resources to pursue travel, fun, creativity, and pursuits that you have postponed all those years of building your business. And you should be prepared for the unexpected challenges of life.

What is involved in your business exit? Should you sell it? Give it to your children or employees? Or close the door and buy an airline ticket?

Are YOU the business? Some individuals create a company that is a job. You may have the personal insight and charisma that attracts clients. Even if you have a webmaster and a book-keeper, you are the business core. If you are that essential, your business may not be highly valued. While you could find another charismatic coach who appeals to your clients, what value would you provide? Why would a coach be willing to pay a hefty fee for a business they could create for themselves?

You might also have a business that hasn't kept up with the times. Not long ago, movie streaming replaced the video rental business. Is new technology changing your business? A valuable business is a "money machine" with marketing, sales, delivery, customer service, and repeat sales systems. The owner can change without impact on the stream of repeat customers. How might you transform your business into a money machine?

Valuing Your Business

When you shift your perspective from seller to buyer, your value consideration changes. An owner knows the effort it takes to build a business. You've made mistakes, pouring money and energy into its growth. You remember your pride on opening day. Like raising a child, no amount of money will compensate you for your years of care.

The buyer's perspective is not as emotional. Your stories may engender a fondness for history, but the business value lies in future profit potential. What systems will continually attract clients? Can ongoing employees keep this ship afloat and sailing into the future? What are future profit projections? Will a new owner require guidance? Will changes be needed for continuing success?

A business valuation provides buyer and seller with a current business worth, including assets, liabilities, and cash flow. Some consider technology, demographics, and competition. Professional valuations can run thousands of dollars, while 25-50% of business owners do their calculation, despite a tendency to over or undervalue your own company. Business exit strategists and business re-sale professionals can assist the business owner in exploring a sale or purchase.

Plan Ahead

Allowing five to ten years for planning can be essential to create systems and increase business value while allowing for any unexpected challenges. Recognize that your exit is inevitable. It WILL happen. The only question is when and under what circumstances.

You may wish to sell your business or pass it to a relative or employee. What are the steps to increase value? How can you multiply your income and reduce your expenses? Can you systemize what works?

- Consider improvements that raise revenue: marketing, sales, production, customer service, referrals
- Provide employee incentives to individuals who are critical to the ongoing success of the company for employee retention.
- Review insurance for protection against loss of property and vital personnel. Protect both property and essential people to protect your overall investment.
- Review your company financial records with your accountant or a business exit strategist. Identify any business owned assets, like automobiles which you will not sell with the business
- If you allow three or more years to improve the business bottom line before a sale, you can grow the value of your business.

As a business owner, you focused on building the business. Planning your exit requires a different lens. Business exit strategists can provide you with a multi-year plan to increase your sale price or terms. These professionals consider how the sale of your business impacts your retirement, estate plan, and legacy.

Consider developing a manual of how your business works with all the contacts, procedures, and systems described in one place. This procedure manual may be the ultimate goal of preparing for a business exit because it enables anyone to continue serving your customers without a hiccup. It doesn't matter whether you are selling your business or transitioning it to a son or daughter. What would happen if you had a severe accident? Even your spouse might need this specific direction to continue the business.

We will all exit our business and this world at some point. That is guaranteed. How can you and your loved ones benefit from your life? That is the question that we will continue in the coming chapters.

KEYS FOR REFLECTION:

This chapter provides ideas for the business owner.

- Starting a business can be an option to earn extra money for retirement, but only if you plan for a successful business.
- Planning for the sale or succession of your business can provide you with the maximum for retirement.

Now it is your turn to journal the following questions:

1. Are you considering building a business? If so, journal your thoughts based upon this chapter.
2. Do you have a business that you could sell? If so,

journal your thoughts on what you might change to improve the value of your company.

3. What other thoughts are arising for you? Do the ideas in this chapter appeal to you or repel you? How does it make you feel? Continue to journal your ideas and feelings until you are complete.

4. What is your action plan to fill any gaps in your financial future? Write down the specifics.

5. Calendar the first step.

Part Three

OPEN YOUR SPIRIT

"It is a waste of time to wish the winds were different. Those who see change coming can adjust quickly and enjoy the ride."
~Carole Hodges

Chapter Thirteen

SURFING CHANGE WITHOUT A BOARD

"You can look at an incoming wave with fear or delight. Why not choose fun and excitement?"
~Carole Hodges

YOU CAN'T FIGHT Mother Nature or the roar of technology. In this time of rapid advancement, your menopause happens with a backdrop of world turmoil. Shifts in your body are genuine and also a wake-up call to the changes all around.

In my days of sailing, I encountered many types of seas. There were days of calm when we cranked up the engine to glide forward. The sea was glass, and we could see the flat circle of each manta ray sunning on the surface. More often, winds blew across the bow. We tightened the sails, zigging and zagging toward our destination. Occasionally, winds came from behind, pushing directly to our goal with our spinnaker to one side while the mainsail and jib balanced the wind on the other. Those were brief moments of joy and ease. Sailors watch the horizon and adapt quickly, knowing that there is little comfort and no benefit to resisting change. Why waste time wishing for kinder winds? Those who anticipate change can adjust swiftly and enjoy the ride.

In this last half of life, we are also sailing unknown waters. This game of life is ours to create a satisfying adventure. We have grown and learned every step of the journey. We face challenges, acknowledging that a higher power guides the outcome. If we live well, we do not always gain control, but we do build resilience. There is no "A" for knowing all the correct answers, but you can play the game like a winner who appreciates outstanding effort and consideration. When you smile at any outcome, you are a winner!

You probably feel change all around. When did you get your first computer? Or your first smartphone, and how have these made your life different? What will that mean for you in the coming years? How will you adapt? More importantly, how will you prosper?

Ours is a world of changing winds. Your skill at adjusting your direction and sails is invaluable. I have always loved the growth of technology, although I have known a world without it. I had one of the first personal computers from Wang that stored and accessed data on tapes. It was slow and required low temperatures to avoid overheating. Next came a Xerox computer with a black screen and green print. I learned to program Fortran and create what we now think of as a simple Excel spreadsheet. I taught companies how to make punch cards to enter data into mainframes for a brief time.

As technology changed, I changed. A friend told me about the new thing called the World Wide Web (WWW) in the early

1990s. Websites gradually became the new thing, and then email. By the end of the nineties, I was a videoconferencing specialist and then a product manager for MCI-Worldcom. I remember getting a call from a new San Francisco company located south of Market to explore partnering with MCI. I met with two young men. They had unusual names, and their goal was to create a world-changing company, but they did not charge for their services. They told me this was called a "search engine." I couldn't make any sense of it. I told my manager that they didn't have anything for us to consider. They had a goofy name... "Google."

Technology may not be readily predictable. New ideas pop up everywhere. Some will take off while others die along the way. Today there are no Wang or Xerox computers, although they had a head start. I didn't understand Google, yet it is now a major technological giant with ever-growing ambition. With over 7 billion people on this planet, over 7 billion brains can improve life beyond our comprehension to understand.

With new technology, opportunities expand. If you plan to work for the next ten years or more, embrace technology that keeps you relevant and competitive. At any age, technology can benefit you. Top financial firms have created software to assist you with investments and money management. Financial firms are also uplifting the education of their workforce to support you in finding long-term solutions.

Our challenge is to bring balance and wisdom to new advances. As a human species, we face endless possibilities. Advanced data analysis can solve human problems while the same data could be harmful and devastating in the wrong hands. We need wisdom, knowledge, and compassion guiding future technology for the benefit of all. I see wise women taking a significant role in this challenge.

It is impossible to track the worldwide plethora of advances. And the rate of change is accelerating beyond our human comprehension. I highly recommend the following book: *The Future is Faster Than You Think: How Converging Technologies Are Transforming Business, Industries, and Our Lives* by Peter Diamandis and Steven Kotler. This book provides an overview of new technology using revolutionary thinking. Companies now look to "10X" their results year over year. Gone is the outdated objective of improving 10% year over year. Exponential growth means breaking traditions and expectations. What will that mean for all of us?

Peter Diamandis originated the X Prize. His organization offers millions of dollars for solutions to seemingly impossible challenges. Winners include:

- Sub-orbital space flight
- Innovative oil spill cleanup
- Tricorder device to "diagnose patients better than or equal to a panel of Board-certified physicians."
- Water Abundance Prize, for a company that successfully extracted over 2,000 liters of water using only renewable energy, at the cost of US$0.02 per liter within 24 hours
- Adult Literacy Prize for a system to improve adult reading literacy within 12 months.

These and more prizes encourage innovative thinking to solve human problems. Independent groups claim more X prizes than existing companies. Previous ways of thinking do not constrain these people, and the results are often remarkable. Powerful computers and 3D printers make it possible for innovators to craft and test solutions faster than ever.

A more philosophical book, *Thank You for Being Late: An Optimist's Guide to Thriving in the Age of Accelerations* by Thomas Friedman, considers the human side of rapid advancement. He questions how humans cope with technology that outstrips their ability to integrate and understand it. The answer may surprise you. It brings us to question the meaning of our humanity and how we create the world that works for all. Friedman highlights our need for deep human connection in caring communities to bring sense to our world. These two books are a wake-up call to our imminent future.

Below are some changes that have already changed our lives and others that will be here within ten years. As you read them, consider how they will impact you. We often think of new technology as pricey. Yet some advances will bring us better service while saving money (think Amazon delivery). You may think you will resist change until it becomes the only sensible solution!

Coming Soon

In recent years, Uber and Lyft transformed the taxi business. They offered a service where riders choose their car and evaluate their driver online before ordering their ride. Using an app to locate their vehicle location in real-time eliminates the foot-tapping frustration of wondering when your ride will arrive. Passengers leave a review, rate drivers, and leave a tip from their smartphone. These quantum improvements to the taxi experience also offer gig income and employment. While not perfect, we now have a new mode of transportation and a source of readily available income.

Electric cars are here and growing. All auto manufacturers now produce these cars, which cost less to drive and reduce or eliminate toxins in the air. The next step is self-driving autonomous cars. They are in test mode worldwide, and the launch of autonomous vehicles is within years in the U.S. and already operating in some locations.

These changes are not occurring because of government regulation or funding. Private companies and investors fund these advancements. Companies know that they will have buyers if reliable, low-cost transportation is available whenever you need it. People will rapidly adopt new technology when the cost of owning, maintaining, and insuring a car is triple the cost of a new offering! The key to any successful business is to magnify quality and shrink cost. Futurists estimate that we will all be using this service by 2030 or sooner.

Imagine how this will benefit seniors who want to be independent but should no longer be in the driver's seat. When self-driving cars are proven, they will expand. Perhaps there will be a service to pick up children from school or to pick up and deliver your groceries. We have an environment where creative minds can thrive.

The first flying car, developed by Hyundai and Uber, is already in use in Dubai. Drones are optimized to drop off deliveries. What will this mean for our lives? Imagine inputting our healthy diet plan to the refrigerator that orders ingredients from a local store and delivers it by drone. Our home robot can then restock the fridge and prepare a meal ready at our designated time. Our home might have access to a personal locator for better timing accuracy. This fantastic world could be closer than you might imagine. The real question is how we will use the extra time in a fully automated world.

Rapid Transformation

2020 stay-at-home orders introduced us to a virtual way of living. Zoom and Microsoft kept a majority of companies operating efficiently, and virtual work is becoming the norm. Productivity increased for some industries during the shutdown. Employees are moving from cities to desirable rural or resort areas, and companies plan to reduce office space. The logic is simple. If all I need is a computer and internet to work, why not live close to recreation? Why not enjoy space and fresh air? Enjoy the true laptop lifestyle!

This change will have ongoing repercussions. What will happen to empty office buildings? Could these become opportunities to create low-cost housing for the homeless? Could these become "vertical farms" to grow food where it is distributed? Could empty offices become art centers or office shares for occasional use? The creative possibilities are endless.

Education came home. Parents and children learned to work together from home. Education became a family affair as never before. We had not anticipated this rapid shift, and the results have been mixed. Separation from friends has been difficult for both children and adults. We are social animals. We like to see, touch, and smell each other regularly. Zoom, Facetime, and

Facebook video messenger improve our remote interaction, but they can't replace the experience of another human being.

A few months ago, I took a continuing education class online. The teacher was captivating, with stories and questions, which kept me involved for over four hours in content that can be technical and tedious. Personal video transforms continuing education into a worthwhile use of time. Before this change, continuing education could be an exercise in boredom, struggling to stay awake while plodding through requirements and hoping to remember details just long enough to take a test.

Recently I spoke with a virtual reality creator. He is a forward thinker, providing simple solutions with a twist. Imagine the thrill of a virtual vacation for seniors confined to nursing homes. A day at the beach might be impossible for these elders. Yet through the magic of a 3D gaming headset, a homebound senior can escape to the beach. She can see the waves and hear the crash of the ocean. With the addition of ocean scent and a sandbox, the senior has a welcome transformation and a sense of freedom.

Virtual reality can blend into daily life. Virtual meeting rooms are a new method for companies to meet from remote locations. These online "rooms" provide the look and feel of being in a live meeting. Gaming technology adapts to real world situations and expands how we interact with others. What ideas might you add?

Education can use a makeover with access to new technology. If we combine the best of virtual and in-person instruction, we might reduce the cost of education. We can eliminate the mountains of student debt that overwhelm many young people while providing quality education for new jobs in our changing world.

Every industry is or will be changing faster and faster. Robots are showing up everywhere to replace humans. We need to reeducate workers at all levels during their working years. Multiple careers are the norm. How does an advanced society plan and deliver ongoing education? Who will provide these solutions for out of the box thinking and innovation? There will be rewards for those who wrangle the answers!

Will Energy Be Free for All?

Are you open to concepts that are beyond our current understanding of how things work? According to Peter Diamandis, "The day before something is a breakthrough; it is a crazy idea."

I am a fan of knowledge. In addition to a fascination with technology, I watch the History Channel enjoying research into ancient sites. Recent breakthroughs in technology now date ancient pyramids worldwide back to 10,000 BC.

What makes this research so interesting is the seeming impossibility of the sites themselves. Construction of the pyramids involved stacking blocks weighing 2-3 tons or more. Slaves supposedly built them without modern equipment. Does it even sound logical that primitive people would decide to use such impossible materials? Even today, we might not be able to replicate the pyramids.

Stonehenge and Gobekli Tepe have multi-ton flat stones capping vertical stones. How did they accomplish that task without modern tools? Our traditional historical narrative leaves inexplicable gaps because primitive people could not have achieved such technologically superior results. Studying ancient sites may uncover advanced, forgotten technology.

In 1901, Nicola Tesla conducted an experiment to demonstrate wireless energy transmission. At Wardenclyffe, Long Island, he erected a 187-foot tower intending to transmit energy wirelessly. Some archaeologists speculate that Nichola Tesla's gleaned his understanding of energy from studying the pyramids. Tesla believed that the pyramids tapped into the naturally occurring magnetic energy field around Earth, and their power may have charged alien spaceships or powered sophisticated tools. He designed the Wardenclyffe tower to emulate early technology to distribute free energy to all. However, financial support for Nicola Tesla dried up when investors realized that they had no way to bill users for this power. Today, we all carry around electronic devices which require energy. We have wires and plugs to power our phones, tablets, personal devices, and laptops. Soon our cars will all require continuous energy. What if abundant free energy could power it all? How might that change the world?

Moments ago, I received my daily copy of "Futureloop," a newsletter put out by Peter Diamandis. The topics bring you a preview of the not-too-distant future:

- **"Urban airport will pave the way for flying cars"** – Coventry's new location is the next step for reducing traffic by putting some in the air.
- **"Virgin Hyperloop Passenger Experience vision is now more realistic"** - Richard Branson's hyperloop will be above ground and using vacuum modules

instead of Elon Musk's boring project, which puts a super-fast train underground.

- **"MIT researchers develop a new 'liquid' neural network that's better at adapting to new info"** – More advancements in artificial intelligence which enable AI to 'learn' more quickly.
- **"Dutch Navy invests in INTAMSYS 3D printers for on-demand spare parts"** New opportunities for 3D printing parts are solving problems.
- **"FINESSE is the innovative new brand using artificial intelligence to disrupt fashion"** AI and social feedback guide fashion design to minimize waste.

Additional articles discussed self-driving busses; growing killer cells to stop cancer growth; printing rockets for space exploration, and Cloud computing from space.

NASA is now taking applications from people who want to be part of the first Earth settlement on Mars. In 2022, cargo ships will start bringing supplies to Mars. The first four space crew will land there in 2024, and by the 2030s, they anticipate sending teams on the 16-month journey to Mars. We are learning along the way. The challenge of living on another planet could provide new ideas for living well here on Earth. When we stretch our boundaries and think outside our proverbial box, we get surprises. Some of these are likely to expand our knowledge.

Wonder Woman Reality

One day I had the opportunity to unleash my superpowers. I live in Fallbrook, which is a small, unincorporated city near San Diego, California. Each year, Fallbrook residents elect an honorary mayor to represent their local Chamber of Commerce for events. Their election is not done by vote but by raising funds for the Chamber and local charities.

I had just arrived in Fallbrook six months before the election. I didn't know many people but thought it might be fun to run for honorary mayor and participate in the community. Once I realized that it was a fund-raising effort, I felt comfortable. I could raise money from any source. It didn't matter that I was a local unknown.

On the 4th of July, there was a massive picnic with food, entertainment, and fireworks. Thinking this would be a great place to raise money, I dressed for the occasion as Wonder Woman. Once I put on the costume, I shifted into superhero mode.

I began to breathe deeply and stand erect. The pose came naturally; feet apart, hands-on-hips, scanning the horizon for dangers. As I walked into the picnic area, my husband asked if I would like a glass of wine. "No," I responded. "I'm Wonder Woman."

Just like that - my persona shifted. All afternoon, young girls came up to meet me and get pictures. I had the girls stand with me, hands-on-hips, chin up, smiling, and ready to take on the world as superheroes. That afternoon, I was bringing feminine power to Fallbrook. I didn't win the honorary mayor position, which went to a lifelong resident, but I made a difference that day.

Shifting to confidence and action can be just that fast and effective. You don't need a Wonder Woman costume. You only need to embrace a seed of passion and let it grow in your heart. A delightful aspect of aging can be a release from concern about the opinions of others.

For years after my Wonder Woman appearance, people have told me, "I can't believe how bold you are...I could never do that." The reality is simple. We all wear clothes every day which express our personalities without even blinking. I've discovered that you can take ANY outfit and label it your "Wonder Woman" armor. The change within is no more than breathing in self-confidence and filling yourself with love and compassion. Once you fall in love with the goodness of your fellow man, you are invincible. It doesn't matter that some people won't understand. None of us need universal approval. When you are clear on what is important to you and how you want to live your life, you are free to be expressive.

Tell people that you care about them. Listen to your own heart and focus on what lights you up. If you are not sure, experiment with people. Look for opportunities to give sincere compliments. Listen carefully to understand what is important to others. Have you ever felt alone in a crowd? In this world of smartphones and digital distraction, people may be physically together yet miles apart in their human connection. Emotional distance vanishes when someone takes the time to listen. You can make that difference once you decide to ask questions and listen. You don't need to say anything profound; just be there for others.

Imagine what will happen when planes can fly faster than the speed of sound, taking you from Los Angeles to Paris or Australia within an hour or two. How will that change your ideas about where you wish to live? Would you choose to live in a different part of the world if your family could still get together quickly? Advances in technology expand our choices.

What will we need to understand to live in a more advanced world? My mother, at age 85, insisted on learning the computer. She went to classes and mastered email, remembered to check on her investments at Charles Schwab, and taught herself how to play cards with opponents worldwide. Computer Bridge became Mom's favorite activity when she couldn't sleep at night. There was always someone in the world available.

Anti-aging research is exploding. It is no longer funded exclusively by governments and is subject to public scrutiny. Google began a project called "Calico" to combat the "disease of aging." We don't know the details yet. Rumors are that Google is experimenting with new drugs to stop and even reverse aging. What might that mean to you and me? If they succeed, what will we choose? It might be wonderful to feel great in our later years and share our wisdom with others. But what about finances? What will it cost to live indefinitely? Might it mean that everyone will anticipate holding a job for their entire lives? Would that eliminate the old-fashioned idea of retirement? What happens to the population of the earth if people live indefinitely? Perhaps we will move to Mars or even other galaxies!

The possibilities are mind-boggling. Without AI-enhanced brains, our generation might become the Neanderthals of a space-traveling age and written up in the history books. That would be a sad way to make history. What do you do when the future is a mind-numbing blur?

Personal Resilience

Could we learn to take life as it comes, and initiate changes as required? Some people are vital and enthusiastic at 80 to 90 years and beyond. What makes that possible? I call it personal resilience, which is an attitude of youthful acceptance.

Personal resilience requires flexibility in the face of change. When you are a baby, you are exceptionally resilient. Babies have no preconceived ideas of what will happen next. They know when they are hungry, or cold, or wet. She is aware of what she needs, even when this little child doesn't know who or how she will get help. Babies are open to receiving care for what they need. As they grow, they develop more preferences.

I wish we could visit and discuss the many ideas in this chapter. If you follow technology, you may have examples I haven't mentioned. Or you may be wondering if I am hallucinating. Change is accelerating, and it can be uncomfortable or exciting. At this point in history, you may not have an option to rely on old ideas of your youth. Yet with awareness of changes, you earn the freedom to choose. If you are imaginative, you can choose to participate. You might create new products and take advantage of opportunities that others don't see.

Take your time to explore your vision of change. Journal your feelings.

KEYS FOR REFLECTION:

How do you feel about the change in your life?

1. What do you need to be resilient in the face of change?
2. Who in your life can be a support in the face of change?
3. Who in your life will need your help to face change?
4. Do you recognize any opportunities for you in coming change?

Chapter Fourteen

COMING OF AGE

"You must find the place inside yourself where nothing is impossible."

~Deepak Chopra

MENOPAUSE IS your second coming of age. You came of age the first time as a young girl in a developing body. Once again, your body is announcing a significant change in your life and identity. Your second coming of age is a recognition of your wisdom and experience. Today, your world is shifting more rapidly than your body. Your place in this world is essential.

Well-trodden beliefs disintegrate as we travel super-highways of rapid advancement. We need wisdom from women who awaken to this calling. None of us can push this monstrous ship of change in a new direction alone. But each of us has a role.

As you face the second half of your life, you bring experience. You have a unique perspective based upon your challenges, passions, and interests. What will you do with your one wonderful life? I admit to my bias. I would like to see every woman come alive by age 50 and step into leading her family, community, country, and the world to become a more loving and supportive place for all. If that feels too daunting, you can relax. Changes begin with just one person, and that person is YOU. Remember, you are not alone. Women all around will join you. The time is right for us to come together.

Step into Wisdom

Every morning you awake to a new day. Every morning you energize your day with feelings that give you the oomph to take on the day. Your emotions get you moving. They get your blood moving, so you take action to make a difference that day. What kinds of feelings do this?

In the last year, we have seen angry exchanges all around. Social media, news, and even family gatherings became opportunities to correct the opinions of others. Why did typically peace-loving people find themselves yelling and getting red in the face? The answer is surprising. People get angry because it gives them satisfaction. What happens when you get mad? Your body moves out of the pre-frontal cortex control, which is generally calm and even-tempered.

"When our brain detects stress — like when we get upset reading a news story or watching a political debate — it diverts oxygen and glucose from the prefrontal cortex to the amygdala, triggering the body's fight-or-flight response. The hypothalamus tells our adrenal glands to pump

stress hormones — cortisol and epinephrine — to prepare our bodies to fight or run. These hormones make our hearts race, blood pressure increase, skin feel hot, and muscles tense."

~ Good Housekeeping, August 20, 2020, by Stephanie Anderson Witmer

When you break down the components of anger, you find energy. We need to get moving because we have decided to fight rather than flee. We are triggered by our hormones and by moral rectitude. As "deep fakes" began to show up in social media, people of all persuasions were angered and ENERGIZED.

Ideas divide and bring the energy of anger. When you feel you are "right," step into the ring to prove it. However, there is another route to self-energizing, which is through ideals.

When we consciously adopt a mission and a vision, we see the potential to make the world a better place. Unlike the energetic spike of anger, we feel a growing sense of hope. We recognize that we need the agreement and support of others to create solutions that work for all. Ideals bring people together. We might not know all the answers when we begin, but we can find solutions by asking questions. How can we ensure:

- Everyone who wants/needs a job can find one?
- That all people have access to primary medical care?
- Basic human needs like food and shelter are available for everyone?
- That all children receive care and education?

What ideas would you add? Should there be standards for our food, water, and air? How do we maintain safe communities? Can we find the root cause of homelessness or poverty? What would make our life adventure more fulfilling and enjoyable? Anger fuels us but solves nothing. IDEAS can divide us – IDEALS gives us another path. Perhaps it is time for soup.

Have you heard the story of *Stone Soup*? Several strangers came to a small town. They were hungry but did not know anyone and had no money. They were creative and had a plan which would benefit everyone who participated. First, the strangers built a small cooking fire in the town square. As curious citizens gathered, they announced that they would share Stone Soup with the community that night. First, they needed a large pot and some water. One neighbor offered the large pot full of water as their contribution. The strangers found several stones and put them into the massive caldron to begin warming. All day, curious people paused as they walked past to ask what was cooking.

"Stone Soup," the visitors answered, "If you add something to the soup, you can share it." Because the visitors were friendly, open, and helpful, people began to add to the soup. They brought carrots, potatoes, peas, chicken, herbs, onions, and more. The pot filled and began to send a wonderful fragrance throughout the town. At dinner time, everyone came with a bowl to taste the Stone Soup. Sure enough, the soup was a hit with the townspeople. They enjoyed visiting with their neighbors and were open to learning more from their new visitors. That day the town discovered the power of contribution. All contributed what was available to them, and the result was extraordinary.

It took two strangers who had a vision and were willing to provide belief and direction. They watched all day to ensure that only good food went into the pot. They would have stopped anyone from dropping dirt into the soup. The truth is that a vision held by someone willing to promote and protect that vision can succeed. Genius and wealth are not required, but persistence, influence, and persuasion are the valuable gems that create change.

If you were contributing to the Stone Soup in your community, what would you bring? Consider what you DO offer to your community. Might it be your creativity? Or good nature? Do you share your enthusiasm or acknowledge people with praise? Perhaps you bring leadership or clarity? What inspires you to speak up? What calls for your participation?

Your New Reality

When I speak with women who are entering the second half of life, I hear similar stories. Like the refrain of a familiar song, it repeats again and again. Life is different because I am different! "One day, I just couldn't put up with the B.S. anymore." "One day, I needed freedom to be myself." "One day I discovered that money alone wouldn't bring me happiness." "One day, I couldn't stand my job...or my husband...or my choices."

That day can be a dramatic departure from your past. Or it can be a fragrant breeze of enticing change which makes you look in a new direction. You may glance at your compass and realize that you are no longer on course. The shift is unexpected and can be frightening. Let me provide the reassurance that you are not alone. As your body and your world change, you transform day by day into a wiser woman.

Neither age nor experience alone endows wisdom. We all know those who are assaulted by each advancing year and cling to the past patterns. Proper understanding accepts change and molds it into a pleasing shape that improves the moment. Wisdom finds joy in the moment, and shares love freely with those in her path. The wise woman is confident enough to offer a stone to start a pot of soup. When she takes the lead, others follow.

Now is a time to be kind to yourself and release judgment. When I was 20, I thought that I would have life tamed into submission by age 50. Had I remained clueless, perhaps I could have pounded my values into stone for posterity? However, life is not as simple as I had imagined so long ago. I became honest with myself, acknowledging that each new day brings fresh adventures. You get real treasure when you combine a wealth of experience with the forgiving eyes of a child. That attitude is worth the quest.

Life Purpose Defined

Begin with self-reflection. Step out of the hurry-scurry of your busy life to consider what you have learned. What challenges have you overcome? Where have you succeeded? What feels complete? What is still yours to conquer? How do you access the strength and courage to move forward?

Self-reflection and connecting to your purpose are never "one and done." If you began a daily journal while reading this book, you might have started to discover the value of this practice. Keeping a regular journal provides a record of your mindset and advancement. I have found that daily journaling offers a point of reference. You can be more honest when it is a habit that doesn't depend upon your mood. If you skip some time, give yourself a pass and simply start in again when you can. Over the years, I have been interrupted by projects, or vacation trips, or work. Life happens. But there is a benefit to returning to my journal.

Reconnect with your heart and soul by making a list of 100 things that you would like to do, visit, accomplish or create in your life. Building your list of 100 is a great exercise to do once every few years. You can post your list or put it on a shelf. When you plan vacations or decide how to reward yourself for an accomplishment, look at your list. Each year you might decide which items you intend to check off that year.

It is not easy to list 100 items. You may find that you are stretching to fill up the lines. That is normal. And the stretch to record 100 wishes will expose more of your true self. I always find that with the grand dreams, like visiting the pyramids in Egypt, I might post a silly wish like taking my best friend to have chocolate gelato on the beach.

As you list your 100 wishes, be sure that you are smiling. All 100 items should delight your spirit. Remember the little girl that once was you? What did she like? Have you wanted a cat? Or to dress as Wonder Woman for a community celebration? Remember – you may never DO everything on your list. (Or maybe I'm just projecting because I haven't done everything on my list.) The point is to focus on what would make this human adventure a real kick in the pants! Have fun framing your future.

As you share your deepest thoughts and dreams with yourself, you will recognize your direction and purpose. Let these thoughts influence your day-to-day choices, and soon you will find that you are enjoying life more. Just keep it up, and up you go!

Profound Sufficiency

Sit with your bucket list. Put a star by the non-negotiable priorities and ask yourself, "How CAN I make this happen?" Are you willing to make changes? Might you have to change your current living style? If you were bold and changed your career, would it fulfill your wishes? What values are important to you? Who are you becoming as you move in the direction of your life adventures?

I have met women who scooped up all their experience, set a firm path on their vision for making the world a better place for humans, and started a new business. They went bold. They went big. They had nurtured their infant idea until it was ready to launch. And they launched with a clear vision and investor funding.

Your bucket list might also be a clue to achieving your highest state of mind and money, giving you a sense of satisfaction. Lynne Twist calls this "profound sufficiency," which is far more than minimalism. "Profound sufficiency" imparts a sense of freedom with your time, activity, and life purpose. You have the means to feel fully expressed, valuable and happy. Imagine life without scrambling for more or doubting your supply of food or shelter. Who would you invite to share your life? Who would be in your community?

When you plan the second half of your life, you are doing much more than helping yourself. When you feel secure within yourself, you can make a more significant difference. When you identify your purpose and align your financial goals to support you, there is comfort and freedom to be fully expressed. This sense of fulfillment is my hope for you.

- Take care of your body and your health
- Create a clear vision of your life and purpose
- Be fully expressed and authentic in your relationships
- Understand your financial need for profound sufficiency
- Create your future by exploring your financial options before retirement
- Create a plan to build and manage your financial future
- Eliminate the specter of fear – there is enough
- Embrace the changing future and explore the possibilities
- Identify ways that you bring wisdom to your community
- Own your creativity, leadership, power – Own your JUJU
- Build a safety net of support
- Reward yourself along the way

Define your purpose and live it:

- What truly matters
- Go with what you know
- Be willing to shift and learn
- Work with others

Learning to trust yourself is a process. I still doubt myself. That is, I don't trust myself until I remember that Spirit is guiding the journey, and all is well. It doesn't matter what it looks like to anyone else. We came for a reason. We came to have an experience that is uniquely ours. Every challenge opens another door of opportunity.

Here you are at mid-life when you can take score. Are you ahead at half-time? Or do you need to catch up and take the lead? What position are you playing? Do you need to make a switch? Where do you want to end up?

We have been on quite a journey through these pages. Yet this is only the beginning for you. My sincere wish for you is to build security both within yourself and within your finances, releasing you to live fully. When you feel good, you can do good.

Money is a form of energy. You see it around you in so many ways. Those that emit positive, sweet energy attract good things. Those who fill up with the energy of power may attract money but miss the possible happiness and connection.

Menopause is a pivotal time in your life as you shift into the finale of this lifetime. You have developed yourself as an individual, and I believe it is your time to shine. But you know that you have your responsibility in creating the outcome.

Why not resolve to make this one incredible life of yours into the best it can be? Suppose you will explore your passions and take the time to make decisions that are consistent with your happiness and joy. In that case, this can be the start of something BIG! You can be a Menopause Millionaire with financial, emotional, and spiritual wealth. Could you discover profound sufficiency which gives you the foundation for a great life?

Stepping Into Wisdom
by Carole Hodges

I have come far
Leaving mountains of regret and rocky mistakes,
Lingering in fields of sweet, smiling memory.
I alone chose roads leading me here.

Facing a sea of endless potential while
A fog of confusion holds me motionless.
Sand supports my feet like earth-bound life crushed into
   tiny grains
Comfort surrounds me - Yesterday dissolves
Flowing through my fingers.

I stand in the ocean foam of possibility.
NOW
Waves caress the beach
Each footprint dents wet sand
Disappearing in the frothy surf
Breathing comfort and assurance
I welcome the moment
NOW!

Resources

Thank you for reading The Menopause Millionaire. We hope the process has given you new insight into the meaning of your life. I intend to support you in your life adventure.

To explore further, join a supportive community, and discover additional resources, join the Menopause Millionaire page on Facebook.

FIND RESOURCES TO SUPPORT YOU AT

www.MenopauseMillionaire.com/resources

APPENDIX 1

A Short History of Money

Imagine a life without money. Historians tell us that forms of money, such as coins, appeared around 600-700 B.C. in Lydia and China. Before that time, experts assumed that barter was the only means of exchange.

People didn't need money to survive. As people reached adulthood (probably at 10 or 12), they got busy creating value. Perhaps they learned a craft or farming or hunting. Maybe they learned to build houses or sing and dance to engage others. Quite simply, they had to learn essential skills and contribute to others. There was no need for money to live. Everybody contributed something. In the process, they also learned about supply and demand. If you had only one thing to trade, you must find a market for it. Even in the world of barter, there were market trends. If too many people had eggs to trade, the value of eggs would decrease.

It was a simpler time. Barter trading worked well because people did not travel far, knew their neighbors, and supported their local community. As people developed an interest in travel, they began trading with people in other countries, and the concept of money was born. Traders used coins and later banknotes. Civilizations which traded were far more sophisticated. They could enjoy products from other countries. They could also produce more of a single item and sell it in another country as an exotic import. Trading built wealth. People worked together to make it happen. A trader would purchase quantities of skins, tools, fabrics, and more. He would hire a ship and load up his goods for sale. If he survived the winds and the waves, he would sell his products in a far-off land. With the money in his possession, he might buy items in a foreign country to make the return trip with him. Once home, he would sell his bounty and get ready to repeat the journey. It was a good way for an adventurous trader to build a fortune. Since he collected his payment in coins and banknotes, he could easily purchase whatever he needed with his "money."

This early "paper money" was not printed by governments as it is now. It was a "banknote" because a private bank issued it. People were taking the word of the bank that they would receive value. Then governments printed and controlled the money. China was the first country to print and distribute currency in 1023 A.D. Much later, in 1690, the Massachusetts Bay Colony printed the first money in the United States to pay soldiers who fought in military action against Canada. The soldiers could take these notes and purchase goods with them.

In 1775, the Continental Congress copied this strategy and printed paper currency to pay soldiers. Unfortunately, they printed so much cash that the notes quickly became worthless. People determine the value of money by their willingness to utilize it. When overprinted, it became useless.

Do you wonder what our money is worth today? Today, in 2021, the United States is making numerous disbursements of checks to alleviate the financial pain of people laid off from their jobs. Could we be making our money worthless? The answer is not quite that simple. Money has an energetic spirit. Let's dive deeper into history.

Until the early 1900s, states had independent banking systems. That changed with the Bank Panic of 1907 when a rush on the banks essentially put the United States at the mercy of the influential banker, JP Morgan. To ensure that our country would never owe its economic survival to a private banker, Congress created the Federal Reserve in 1913, passing the Federal Reserve Act. The FED became America's National Bank to oversee the United States money supply and ensure stability.

That raises the question, "what is financial stability?" On the national level, the goal of the Fed is to keep both inflation and unemployment low. The FED controls the interest rate and monitors or increases the money supply. When many of our citizens do not have enough money to buy food, we have instability. We recognize that people without the essentials to survive will fight to live. In 2020, a vast number of people were without jobs and reliant on food lines. The government released up to $1400 per person to those earning under $75,000 based upon the previous year's income. While the criteria for distribution were not perfect, economic urgency required a speedy response. How is this different from another financial anomaly in our recent past?

The last major economic challenge was the Great Recession, lasting from December 2007 to June 2009. During that time, we experienced runaway pricing on homes as a result of subprime lending. Subprime lending, also known as "liar's loans," allowed buyers to proclaim their income without proof. This practice permitted unqualified borrowers without adequate income to make payments, to obtain mortgages. Home prices escalated 25% per year. Sub-prime home buyers were optimistic that the massive increase in home values would allow them to buy a home, live in it for a few years, and then sell it. They anticipated that increased home value would give them a windfall profit. To many, it made sense, and it appeared that everyone was doing it.

Then Wall Street got involved. They could make MORE money available for subprime loans via hedge funds. Here is how that cycle works:

- Initially, a bank lends money to a homebuyer. Then the bank sells the mortgage to Fannie Mae, which gives the bank more funds to make additional loans.
- Fannie Mae then packages a group of mortgages to resell on the secondary market. These mortgage bundles appealed to hedge funds.
- A hedge fund would buy a mortgage bundle and get creative. The mortgage-backed security (MBS) was divided into portions based on risk. For instance, the 2nd and 3rd years of interest-only loans are riskier since they are further out, and there is an increased possibility that the homeowner will default, but it provides a higher interest rate. Sophisticated

computer programs calculated the figures. By splitting a single mortgage into multiple investment segments and then bundling with other mortgages, it became impossible to track the ownership of a single mortgage. A diverse group of people owned portions of each home mortgage.

- As owners defaulted, the problems accelerated. A bank collecting payments might evict the defaulting owner, but the house could not be resold because ownership of the home was not definitively established.

As underlying home values decreased and increasing interest rates triggered mortgage defaults, the US fell into a significant recession.

These bundles were called "derivatives." As owners defaulted, banks foreclosed on large numbers of homes, posing as the lender. The actual owners were the groups of derivative holders. However, the ownership portions were diluted and distributed. There was no practical way to identify the holder of the note. Families lost their homes, and with no clear title, the hedge fund investors could not recover their investments. It was a losing situation all around. Homeowners, investors, and banks all lost.

The Great Recession was a demonstration of money madness. Greed kills the healthy spirit of money. The easy money policies that supported "liar loans" and hedge fund creativity were a disaster. The unfortunate folks who believed that real estate could continuously increase 25% per year were punished for their folly by foreclosure. And many folks got caught in the whirlpool and lost their jobs. The Great Recession, which officially lasted from December 2007 to June 2009, pushed the US unemployment rate to a peak of 10.6% in January 2010.

As you read the last few paragraphs about the Great Recession, what is your perspective? While some people profited from either real estate or investments during this time, others lost homes or jobs. And some stayed on the side-line because it looked crazy. Do you fit any of these categories? How do you make sense of it?

Money Distribution

Can we agree that money is not always predictable? Some investments can be guaranteed, but even that is relative to inflation or deflation. Money changes.

In the last twenty years, we have experienced another change that goes largely unmentioned. The distribution of wealth is undergoing significant change.

Based upon the Federal data available in October 2020, the top 1% of Americans have a combined net worth of $34.2 trillion which is 30.4% of all household wealth in the US. According to the same study, the bottom 50% of the population holds $2.1 trillion, 1.9% of all household wealth.

Let that sink in:

- The top 1% hold 30.4% of the wealth.
- The bottom 50% have 1.9% of the wealth.
- The wealthy are getting wealthier while the bottom 50% are falling behind.

What does that mean to you? Are there evil forces at work? Is this a credit to the genius of the few? Or is it a sign of discrimination and intentional inequality? Is the Fed not doing its job? Will this change? How do we make sense of it?

Let's return to an earlier time to our basic humanity. In the days of the barter trade, we survived without money because everyone recognized that they could exchange their skills and talents. We each have our unique genius and personalities. People didn't get an equal distribution of anything in this human adventure, and money is no exception. Still, we might ask ourselves which principles and actions create the best outcome for ourselves and others. Is there a connection between our success and the well-being of others?

What happens when the concentration of wealth collapses into 1-2% of the population as it has today? The Economic Policy Institute (EPI) offers multiple reports that confirm this dramatic shift in wealth that began in the 1970s. Their studies measure the scope of the problem but define neither the cause nor the solution.

When you look at a list of the wealthiest Americans, you will see familiar faces from the world of technology (Jeff Bezos, Elon Musk, Bill Gates, Mark Zuckerberg, Larry Ellison, Larry Page, Sergei Brin). These men understand the acceleration of knowledge and artificial intelligence (AI), which outstrips our human ability to parse data and uncovers new solutions to our problems. How will AI impact our future?

Some technology improves our lives. Over the past twenty years, Amazon has become a household word. The company can deliver nearly any product known to man in record time – and they continue to improve. Jeff Bezos, the founder of Amazon, earned his place in the 1% of wealth by developing a revolutionary distribution model. He provides convenience at a discount which benefits everyone. We reward people who make a massive difference in our economy. Yet, I wonder if there could be another wealth model?

How do we address the large number of people struggling for the basics of life? Disease put many people out of work through no fault of their own. The vast divide between the 1% and the 50% grows even more prominent as we watch. If you are doing well, perhaps you never address this situation. But the spirit of money has its own rules. Money is also called "currency" because it must flow. The velocity of money, which is the rate of flow from person to person, provides prosperity. Money must flow for a healthy economy. When you have money, you can spend it on necessities, fun, or luxuries. When you don't have money, it can't flow. Life becomes stagnant and even frightening. If money must flow (currency), what is the best way to ensure it flows?

If you give money to someone who has few assets and little money, they will buy food, shelter, and necessities. Any cash they receive will return into circulation. If you give money to someone who has financial reserves, they may leave it in their wallet or put it in the bank, which slows the flow. Or they might build a company that creates more jobs and multiply the flow. There is no certainty about the outcome when the wealthy receive money. To accelerate the flow of money, ensure that it moves from person to person rapidly.

Keep this thought for a moment while we introduce another idea about money. For years, economists have evaluated how money works. Their objective is to find the balance that will enable people to thrive. Different economic theories abound.

At one time, gold reserves backed our currency. The gold standard gave people security that our paper dollars were worth a standard amount of gold. The gold standard also contributed to the pain of the Great Depression. At the start of the Depression, the US could not expand its money supply to stimulate the economy because it would need to increase its supply of gold first.

Bank failures alarmed the public, and those who owned gold began to hoard it. In this situation, cash could not circulate, and money could not "flow." In 1933, Franklin D. Roosevelt took the US off the gold standard. The government made it illegal to hold gold, and private citizens were required to sell their gold coins, bullion, and gold certificates for $20.67 per ounce. The gold went to Fort Knox and increased the federal gold reserves of the United States. Gold's value was raised to $35 per ounce and remained at that level until 1971. President Nixon removed the US from an agreement to purchase gold at that price. Since that time, we have had "fiat" currency. It is not backed by a physical commodity but by the strength of the US government that issues it.

Worldwide demand for dollars now supports our dollar. Without going too deeply down the rabbit hole of financial minutia, let's say that it fluctuates.

Modern Monetary Theory

A contemporary theory of economics called "Modern Monetary Theory" (MMT) emerged from the 2007 to 2009 Great

Recession. MMT challenges the common misunderstanding that the Federal budget works like a home or business budget. If you or I borrow money, we understand that we will have a loan that requires repayment. We are familiar with how this works for our household. All fifty states must also balance their budget. Any State that borrows money by issuing bonds must repay the bonds with interest. The Federal Budget does not operate in the same way. A federal government deficit means that the government has spent more than it will receive in taxes. It is an entry on a balance sheet. There is no debt to pay because there was no loan. We do not borrow money from another country, and no automatic tax increases follow. Recent pandemic relief plans distributed money to those earning less than $75,000 and to the unemployed. This distribution increased money flow resulting in a rapid increase in the number of jobs.

At the end of 2020, the federal deficit was $3.1 trillion. Since that time, the government has released an additional $1.9 trillion relief package. A $1.2 trillion infrastructure plan is also under consideration. The reasoning behind these expenditures is that it makes our economy more sustainable, resilient, and just. We need roads, power production, strong internet, clean water, and protection against the ravages of climate change so that our citizens can be productive and thrive. Some spending by the federal government gives American workers jobs and provides the resources for additional employment.

The Deficit Myth by Stephanie Kelton (published by PublicAffairs) provides a well-researched education on how our government distributes money without going into debt. Kelton is a proponent of Modern Monetary Theory (MMT). MMT evaluates the USA monetary history from 1970 to now. She clarifies that the FED, which controls the flow of dollars, has two objectives. First, to eliminate unemployment. Second, to control inflation. In practice, the FED targets an unemployment rate of 2-4% and an inflation rate of $\leq$2%. Stephanie Kelton provides a fresh view of the national economy, from 1971 when Nixon eliminated the gold standard.

In 1970, the world population was 3.68 billion, compared to 7.87 billion in 2019. It stands to reason that a rapid doubling of humans impacts our money supply. Each new human being has potential value, the value they will provide with their unique skills AND their need for food, housing, etc. The world money supply must increase as well. Imagine that each person in the world had $1 in 1970. By 2019, that amount would be less than $.50 if money were stable. The amount of money would be more than double for each person in the world to have $1 today. MMT considers the contribution of people as the source of our actual economy.

The role of the Federal Reserve is to monitor the supply of money and adjust interest rates. Raising interest rates slows the flow of money. Taxation is a tool to take excess money out of the economy to lower inflation. MMT only suggests raising taxes as a method of reducing inflation. *The Deficit Myth* allows you to delve deeper into the Spirit of Money. As you learn, you gain an appreciation of the complexity of money.

We have gone on a journey in this chapter.

- We began with barter and shifted to coins and paper money, from banknotes to government issued.
- We reviewed the basics of the Great Depression and the Great Recession

- We acknowledged the widening wealth divide between the top 1% and the bottom 50%.
- We considered the impact of the gold standard.
- Finally, we learned how Modern Monetary Theory evaluates the federal deficit.

You could study any of these topics in-depth if you are inspired to learn more. We conclude that money is in flux. And we didn't even mention the shift toward digital money!